Positive Parenting for the Explosive Child

The Yell-Free Parenting Guide You Wish Your Parents Had Read! Stop Losing Your Temper Using Behavior Management Tools, and Effective Discipline Strategies

Ashley Hardoon

Contents

Introduction   VII

1. Understanding the Explosive Child   1

2. Creating an Explosive Child   11

3. The Reward System for Behavior Modification   27

4. The Imitation Game   53

5. Protecting Your Vocal Cords!   69

6. Becoming a Better Parent   83

7. Raising an Emotionally-Intelligent Child   95

8. Forming a Well-Knit Parent-Child Relationship   109

Summary   127

Selected References   133

Introduction

No one is ever quite ready; everyone is always caught off guard. Parenthood chooses you. And you open your eyes, look at what you've got, say 'Oh, my gosh,' and recognize that of all the balls there ever were, this is the one you should not drop. It's not a question of choice.
Marisa de los Santos, Love Walked In

How do you define good parenting? What does your dream parent look like? What kind of parent do you strive to be? This book provides some answers to these questions. The end goal is to help you become a "better" parent. Why not a perfect parent? Because nobody knows what a "perfect" parent is! While some people like their kids to behave exactly as they say, others prefer a more laid-back approach and allow their children to make their own choices. Each of these approaches has its pros and cons. So, it is not straightforward to define "perfect parenting." However, even if one tries, aiming for perfection is never a good idea. Instead, you better focus on improving your parenting while keeping your child's best interests in mind.

Like many parents, I have been deep in the parenting trenches for countless days, searching for help and advice to raise my 10-year-old son. He seemed to taunt my authority at every turn, making me more likely to lose my temper. I am a Psychology major. But apparently, that background was not enough to handle the parenting challenges. When he was a toddler, I spent around two years learning and improving my parenting by reading countless books, attending parenting seminars and counseling sessions, listening to parenting podcasts, and practicing my learnings. Everything I learned felt revolutionary then and hooked me on the idea of growing closer to my son through better parenting. I wished I had those tools sooner, but I was grateful I could make a change before it was too late. Finally, I began to sense that I was capable of making a shift away from the toxic parenting of my childhood and just how much my son craved positive interactions with me. My son was capable of being a well-behaved child and developed even more so into a calmer and happier version of himself as my yelling started to dwindle.

Eventually, I took on the training process to become a licensed therapeutic foster parent through our state.

This entailed many training sessions and continuing education credits every few months that taught me the best ways to interact with the children who would come through our home.

As I made the necessary shifts in my parenting strategy, I felt more at peace with myself and my child. My home life began to reflect the more mindful approach I embraced, and things shifted radically. I still made plenty of mistakes along the way that resulted in setbacks to my new parenting practices. Still, I was on my way to breaking the chains of generational toxicity. My mistakes ultimately shaped my experiences and contributed to my growing expertise in the field and my professional learning. I don't want you to go through the same errors I made, so I wrote this book to share what I learned firsthand.

You might be one of those parents that have tried various parenting styles and have received countless pieces of parenting advice but still have daily struggles. You might wonder which parenting style will work for your situation. This question isn't easy to answer because everyone has unique circumstances, and every child is different. I have seen conflicting results in various parenting styles with my kids. Some children react better to clear rules and routines, while others prefer some level of freedom and autonomy. But one thing I know for sure; all children crave love, attention, respect, and love to have connected parents!

In 1967, Diana Baumrind (an American clinical and developmental psychologist) published a paper in Genetic Psychology Monographs to present three main parenting styles: authoritarian, permissive, and authoritative. Since then, several other styles, including neglectful parenting, child-centered parenting, and toxic parenting, have been proposed.

When you ask your child to do something just because "You are the dad (or mom)", you are being authoritarian. Although this style offers clarity regarding the boundaries and the consequences of crossing them, it removes warmth from the parent-child relationship and tends to be inflexible. The opposite of authoritarian parenting is permissive parenting. Here, the child is free to choose, and the parent behaves like their best friend. Such a parent-child relationship could be very nurturing, but it lacks boundaries and fails to teach the child that every choice comes with inevitable consequences.

Authoritative parenting is what most psychologists consider to be the sweet spot. It strikes a good balance between setting boundaries and consequences and offering a safe and warm environment for the child. For example, you are authoritarian if you set a rule and ask your child to obey it, no questions asked. But if you discuss the same rule with your child, explain why you put it, let your child express their ideas, and be flexible enough to let go of the rule if needed, you are an authoritative parent. Also, realize that many parents could start the day authoritatively, and as the day passes and their energy dwindles, they become more permissive. In reality, most parents adopt a combination of multiple parenting styles. What matters is the overall ratio over extended periods.

There are two common threads in defining all parenting styles:

1. How responsive are the parents to their child's needs and interests, and

2. How demanding they are regarding the rules and repercussions.

Balanced parenting and positive parenting (the title of this book) generally overlap with authoritative parenting and try to strike a balance between responsiveness and being demanding. Balanced parenting aims to establish clear rules and consequences while being warm and involved. Positive parenting does the same by focusing on the child's strengths rather than their weaknesses. Hence, some people call it "strength-based parenting."

I have tried many parenting styles with my son and dozens of foster kids in the past ten years and have mentored other parents. In my experience, positive parenting is the only parenting style that can work for all families, regardless of the family size, age of children, socio-economic circumstances, or parent's personality. Let me explain!

Often our natural default approach as a parent (or partner, co-worker, manager, etc.!) is to nit-pick, i.e., we tend to focus on what is wrong, missing, or lacking. This negativity bias is a built-in survival mechanism deep in our subconscious mind to keep us safe. As nit-picking parents, we're keen to focus on what our children do wrong and try to "fix" them. Changing this attitude and shifting our focus to what our kids do right is the central premise of positive parenting.

When you recognize, reward, and reinforce positive behaviors and impulses in your child, you are practicing positive parenting, even if you have never heard the name! Of course, your approach might be slightly different from someone else's. But the central thought stays the same; to have positive and instructive interactions with your child and to offer warmth, empathy, and support.

As mentioned earlier, some people call positive parenting "strength-based" because it focuses on the child's strengths rather than weaknesses. But what is a "strength," and how can you, as the parent, recognize them? Strength is any good behavior or action a child does often, happily, and well. For example, they might be good at a particular sport, painting, or talking. Similarly, they might have certain character traits such as kindness or curiosity. The more you know your child and respect their uniqueness, the easier it will be to discover their strengths.

Positive parenting is inspired by the theories of the Austrian psychotherapist Alfred Adler from the early 1900s. Adler was the founding father of the school of Individual Psychology and created a set of parenting guidance practices based on respect and dignity. He believed once a child's basic needs (e.g., food, clothing, and somewhere to live) are met, every child has two other fundamental needs: to belong and to feel significant. Belonging is feeling connected to the people and the environment around them and wanted by the family members and caretakers. Simply put, belonging is being noticed and getting the love and attention of the people around them. Significance is being able to make choices, have power, and feel that their opinions and preferences matter. Positive parenting tries to satisfy a child's need for attention and power via positive interactions, i.e., by connecting with the child, recognizing their good behaviors, and nurturing them.

You can fulfill your children's need for attention by spending undivided time with them and reassuring them that you love them, or they will get it by whining and throwing tantrums. On the other hand, you can make them feel significant by letting them make daily choices, involving them in making decisions, and empowering them to do age-appropriate tasks, or they will exert power by refusing to comply or talking back on every little thing.

As you can see in the abovementioned examples, positive parenting is proactive; you take action to ward off future misbehaviors. When you address your children's need for attention and power regularly and positively, you minimize the instances in which they try to fulfill their emotional needs by misbehaving. Realize that children will always misbehave from time to time because they are tired, bored, or overwhelmed. But with positive parenting, such moments will gradually diminish.

Positive parenting proponents consider misbehavior a sign and not a problem or issue. Misbehavior is a cry for help; it's the child's way of saying something is wrong. If you meet their emotional needs for belonging and significance, the misbehavior will be largely gone. This focus on basic human needs makes positive parenting valuable for all families.

My take on positive parenting is a methodology to build a relationship with my children that includes caring, teaching, leading, communicating, striking a balance between being firm and compassionate, and establishing a responsive and interactive environment where my children feel appreciated and motivated to thrive. What you read in this book is based on the positive parenting experiences of a foster mom. I aim to share factual and scientifically accurate learnings, tested and proven in practice and relatable for everyone.

In this book, you will discover how to practice positive parenting with a particular focus on raising explosive and easily-frustrated children. The book consists of three parts. The first part introduces the explosive child, their characteristics, and the challenges of raising them. The second part provides various techniques for dealing with an explosive child using reward systems and without yelling. Finally, the third part equips the reader with a powerful toolkit to manage stress, enhance emotional intelligence, and foster a fantastic parent-child relationship.

If your household has become a minefield, where you have to tread slowly and carefully around your little one, lest you don't tick them off and set them into a melt-down, this book will be worth your time. You can expect a quick, informative, and enjoyable read with many tips and tricks to make your parenting life easier! If yelling at your child to discipline them has taken a toll on you and has strained your parental relationship, this book can help you with some of the essential dos and don'ts of parenting to improve your parent-child dynamic.

Fredrik Backman, the Swedish author and colum-nist, has a remarkable observation about parenting in his best-selling novel *Anxious People*:

"Do you know the worst thing about being a parent is? That you're always judged by your worst moments. You can do a million things right, but if you do one single thing wrong you're forever that parent who was checking his phone in the park when your child was hit in the head by a swing. We don't take our eyes off them for days at a time, but then you read one text message and it's as if all our best moments never happened. No one goes to see a psychologist to talk about all the times they weren't hit in the head by a swing as a child. Parents are defined by their mistakes."

Parents who use positive parenting techniques still make mistakes. But they can survive their blunders, bounce back, and keep going because they proactively build a strong relationship with their child. Give positive parenting a shot if you seek mutual respect and wish to enjoy yell-free parenting. Your journey to become one of those exemplary parents starts here (if you have not already started!). Who knows how far you can reach! I hope this book will be your guide and companion along the way. If you enjoyed this book, please submit a review to help future readers like yourself and me as a writer!

Chapter One

Understanding the Explosive Child

*The children who need love the most will always ask for it
in the most unloving ways.*
Russel Barkley

The Explosive Child! It sounds like an old low-budget horror movie you'd put on to watch solely to laugh at its absurdity. But, unfortunately, an explosive child is nothing like that! When it comes to children with negative emotions, such as anger, frustration, and bawling, we are quick to shut them down and put different labels on them; attention-seeking, manipulative, and stubborn. However, we couldn't be more wrong. Your child reacts to routine problems by lashing out, screaming, and crying because they lack the proper skills to deal with their frustrations or to express themselves. A child's explosive nature occurs due to the child experiencing demands and expectations far greater than their capacity to respond adaptively.

An explosive child requires much patience, significantly more than any other child. This is because they lack essential cognitive skills, such as flexibility/adaptability, frustration tolerance, and problem-solving. When placed in situations where such skills are required, they exhibit their frustrations rather explosively. It is a constant battle between these children's expectations and skill sets.

Seeing your child react aggressively towards you is bound to leave parents feeling despondent, especially young parents with no previous experience with children; they're left questioning their parenting skills, and the parent-child dynamic begins to falter. The inability to understand your child can feel despairing. Hence, let's review the reasons behind an explosive child's behavior and whether it's as serious as you think.

Childhood Trauma and Intermittent Explosive Disorder

"The ax forgets, but the tree remembers." One of my favorite proverbs. At first glance, you may not see the insinuation, but once you do, it proves to be a rather woeful realization. Unfortunately, parents and guardians sometimes project their insecurities and generation of hurt onto their children. While they forget, children rarely do, unless they get the proper support system and love, an even rarer occurrence.

Children brought up in households with a history of violence, abuse, and resentment grow up instilled with the same traits. Whether the maltreatment is directed at them or happening around them, children form personalities based on these encounters and eventually develop triggers that go off when their mind senses they could face the same tribulations. These triggers include extremes of anger, exasperation, irresistible aggressive impulses, and repeated sudden episodes of violent behavior. Such an anger issue is called Intermittent Explosive Disorder (IED).

Maltreatment in childhood leads to the development of IED; resulting in children being unable to navigate their minds and feelings without unleashing their wrath and having difficulty communicating with anyone. Explosive children are prisoners of their minds; when experiencing an aggressive episode, they feel not in control and unable to maneuver through the labyrinth that is in their minds.

Children subject to trauma find it difficult not to give in to their destructive behavior, having little to no experience managing their feelings and negotiating interpersonal relationships. This leaves them unable to control their fits of disproportionate anger. But how should parents know when their child's explosive behavior is more than just normal tantrums? Well, let's have a look.

If asked what my utopia would look like, I would, without skipping a beat, wish for quiet calm children; just imagine no tantrums nor any hissy fits. No? Can't imagine? Well, it's a utopia for a reason. Tantrums can be a result of many different things. So, let's review some tantrum triggers.

Young children feeling frustrated with their limitations, angry about not being able to get their way, or just facing difficulty completing a task, will resort to throwing a tantrum and becoming aggressive. They lack the skill set to effectively express themselves and share their frustrations and will thus have a meltdown instead. The unfolding scene can be a scary and stress-inducing experience for you and your child; however, it is crucial that you remain calm and not resort to shouting or screaming, as that would escalate the situation. How you deal with the tantrum also depends on its severity; it is very concerning if your child has turned out to harm you, themselves, or others. Also, if your child's defiance has hindered your family life and has caused conflicts between the family members to the point where it has even brought about internal issues, it is a very worrying matter. If your child's behavior has started causing trouble outside of your home, like at school, on playdates, or at birthday parties, and has caused other children to alienate them, it may be more than typical behavior. It isn't normal that after calming down, they begin to hate themselves and feel they have no control over their feelings.

IED involves reacting to a situation way out of proportion by sudden, random aggressive outbursts and destructive behaviors. While the severity of the outbreaks may decrease with age, it is a chronic disorder that can continue for years. Tantrums and meltdowns become increasingly concerning if the occurrence is higher and happens with greater intensity or past the age when the child is expected to be emotionally mature. Over time, their aggression becomes more dangerous and can become a problem at home, school, or around friends. While there is no panacea for the disorder, with the help of a professional, your child's explosive behavior will diminish, and you will ultimately feel less bothered by your child's rage.

Is your child using anger to control you?

Anger. Frustration. Disappointment. These are all problems that both children and adults go through. Notice how I said problems, not feelings or emotions. That is because when experiencing those feelings, they tend to make poor decisions that only worsen matters. For example, children, lacking a frame of reference for their pains, will feel the world at the brink of its end when denied a piece of chocolate. While some will communicate their concerns and even be willing to compromise, others will participate in a standoff with their parents and threaten to act out and make a scene. Some parents will give in to these threats and succumb to their child's wants; the child will completely shift control to themselves and gain power. If this sounds familiar to you and reminds you of your parenting situation, then you better keep reading! This section discusses how and why children bully their parents by putting them in challenging and embarrassing situations and threatening that they'll lose their temper to gain power over them.

Children will repeatedly participate in this deliberate defiance at home and school if not methodically dismantled. It'll become their primary coping skill, and they will continue to train adults to give them what they want. To prevent yourself from being bossed around by your child and forced to do something, you must stay steadfast in your methodology and not allow yourself to bend to the child's wishes. Eventually, it is crucial to regain your control and power and restore your authority in the relationship.

Children can learn explosiveness from their parents. Parents with IED will reflect their anger on their children. Then, the typical parenting issues such as sleep deprivation, stress, and exhaustion amplify it. When frustrations mix and build up, the only outcome is an explosive cocktail! Yelling at kids models a destructive attitude; that it is OK to vent out frustrations explosively. Yelling parents and explosive children create a vicious circle that takes an enormous effort and awareness to break. In the following chapters, we will discuss knowing your anger triggers, delaying reactions, thinking of yourself as a role model for your child, and many more anger and stress management techniques.

A child needs to be taught that their feelings are valid and understood. Once you relate with your child on that level, they will feel comfortable and calm down to communicate about why they were so upset rather than using their anger to control you. Teaching your child to learn from their negative frustrated emotions will allow them to make the necessary changes to avoid the same instances from occurring again. It shows them they are in control of their feelings, can make decisions, and choose how to learn from their experiences.

Your child should understand their feelings and implement healthier ways to deal with their frustrations. But it is futile if you, as a parent, are not mentally and emotionally ready to take charge and follow your parenting values instead of letting your child's behavior control the situation. So, successful parenting starts with you and not your child!

The life of an explosive child

Symptoms are nature's way of saying, "something isn't right in this body." They're a tell-tale sign to indicate the presence of something foreign, something that shouldn't be there. And while IED is a mental illness that the naked eye can't see, signs and symptoms allow one to understand one's behavior and get help accordingly.

An intermittent explosive disorder episode has no fixed time; when it happens, it will be sudden and random. While some have episodes daily, others stay nonviolent for weeks and months. A typical episode lasts for about 30 minutes. The main sign of this disorder is unnecessary outbursts of anger in situations that did not ask for that aggressiveness. While people with IED are aware of their destructive behavior, they feel unable to control themselves. These aggressive outbursts can cause significant distress and eventually lead to problems at school and home. The anger manifests as property damage, for instance, breaking objects and slamming doors. Other forms include domestic violence, road rage, physically assaulting people and animals, and getting into verbal arguments.

Before an IED episode, a person will experience sudden rage and frustration, irritated by human touch, and a mind scattered with different thoughts. First, one feels high energy levels, a tight chest, followed by tingling in the arms, legs, and hands. Then, a rhythmic shaking movement comes onto the arms, legs, and hands, and the heart rate increases considerably. After the outburst, a sense of relief washes over the person, followed by regret and embarrassment.

As parents, it is vital to think realistically and set your expectations accordingly. So while we've discussed when temper tantrums can become a cause of concern, we will now go through when you can expect your child to have these meltdowns in the first place. As mentioned in the Introduction, all children need attention and power. When these emotional needs are not fulfilled, they misbehave.

Usually, around 18 months, toddlers will begin to present signs of temper tantrums. This can include but is not exclusive to biting, hitting, and screaming. Since children cannot articulate themselves when feeling immense frustration, the inability to express themselves causes them to lash out in such a way.

Without establishing a mindset to understand why your child is behaving so explosively, you can never help them improve. However, if you strategize to learn about the causes of explosiveness, you'll be better equipped to handle your child's behavior and ultimately form a loving and healthy parent-child dynamic.

Explosiveness sows seeds of insecurity, uncertainty, and terror in the child. Secondly, experiencing trauma impairs the child's cognitive development and emotional stability; when faced with adversity, they initiate a toxic stress response. Finally, trauma also causes the child to become socially stunted and diminishes their ability to engage in normal day-to-day life, partake in school effectively, and initiate healthy interpersonal relationships.

Children show oppositional, non-compliant, and defiant behaviors for various reasons; childhood trauma, lack of cognitive skills, seeking attention and power, modeling angry and explosive parents, etc. Positive parenting provides valuable tools to address most of these reasons. As mentioned before, the misbehavior of a child is a cry for help, it's a symptom and not the root cause. Sometimes parents create and nurture defiance through their parenting mistakes. Over time, the child learns how to exert power and seek attention by talking back, arguing, physical aggression, and similar behaviors. The best strategy to deal with an explosive child is not making one in the first place! How? Start with eliminating some of the most typical parenting mistakes. It is unrealistic to talk about positive parenting and building a solid parent-child relationship while the parent regularly makes mistakes. We'll discuss these typical mistakes in Chapter 2. Then continue replacing the misbehaviors with good behaviors, as explained in Chapters 3 and 4.

The upbringing of an explosive child is daunting; there will be days when nothing seems to work; your children will sometimes refuse to cooperate and completely shut down. Some days they'll lash out, and their anger will push your emotional buttons, maybe to the point where you'll give in and try to appease them. Or even worse, you'll try to intimidate and punish the child for scaring and training them to behave better. You don't want to get into a battle for power with your child, and in the next chapter, I will explain why, so let's keep going!

Chapter Two

Creating an Explosive Child

So much is asked of parents, and so little is given.
Virginia Satir

Are explosive children born that way or conditioned to behave explosively over time? I have worked with many foster kids; admittedly, some were much harder to handle than others. So, maybe some children are born with particular traits that make them more irritable or defiant. But how about the environment and parenting? We know that children mirror their parents' actions and reactions. So, how we parent our children certainly contributes to their behavior. This chapter discusses how defiant and explosive children are made and how parental mistakes contribute to this process.

Making of a defiant child

I'm sure many parents, including me, are guilty of comparing and wondering why their child is so hard to deal with. So it is not surprising for parents who find themselves incredibly frustrated and drained when coping with their child's disruptive behavior to question why their child is always the one to lash out and is so difficult to manage. Young children with their limited vocabulary face great difficulty expressing their frustrations. Unable to communicate with their parents, it is probable to resort to anger, defiance, and irritability when overwhelmed.

Lack of control in a child's day-to-day life can also contribute to them being argumentative and refusing to comply. While many kids don't mind, some even enjoy the decisions made for them, and others can find it confining. Again, this can result in the child defying to achieve some sort of control over their life. "It's just a phase." While this can be said about a child with a challenging temperament, it is an entirely different case for persistent and frequent forms of defiant behavior, known as Oppositional Defiant Disorder (ODD). ODD describes a pattern of irritable moods, unruly behavior, and spitefulness that can last up to six months. For children younger than five, the disorder can occur almost daily; however, its occurrence decreases to at least once a week with time.

A child who loses their temper quickly becomes unusually sensitive and bores resentment toward his surroundings is likely to suffer from ODD. In addition, they will become argumentative and refuse any authority. While it is normal for most kids to behave defiantly, depending on the severity of their defiance, it is important to evaluate whether their outbursts contain specific patterns. This will be the deciding factor in knowing whether ODD is making your child behave so defiantly. It is essential to keep in mind as parents and guardians that when a child is non-compliant, their intentions aren't to frustrate you. Instead, all they seek is to feel significant in that moment.

Common parental mistakes with explosive children

Dealing with an explosive child who refuses to cooperate even the slightest bit can be draining and overwhelming, causing you to make mistakes when approaching the child. Here are some of the common mistakes made by parents of difficult and explosive children:

Mistake 1: Engaging the child's tantrums

"One of the greatest gifts you can give someone is the gift of attention." No offense to Jim Rohn, but when it comes to children putting up a tantrum, giving the gift of attention is not a good idea! Any positive and negative attention is gratifying to a child, and they will do right about anything to receive it, whether it's doing chores or having a breakdown in a public place to get their way. Parents usually face no issue with singing the praises of their children; it's when parents are met with temper tantrums and defiant behavior they begin to scratch their heads.

When parents engage with their children during their tantrums, they may unknowingly reward the behavior and increase the odds of it happening again. How you respond to your child's defiant behavior can impact the likelihood of that behavior occurring again. For nonviolent outbursts, the goal is to ignore the child and withdraw all attention; even negative attention, like reprimanding or persuading the child, reinforces the behavior.

When you engage with your child's tantrums, you inadvertently teach them that meltdowns work; they will adopt this as a skill and use it to get what they want because, from their experience, it has never failed and ultimately resulted in their gain. Therefore, you should withhold attention from such outbursts and discourage defiant behavior. Instead, appreciate and look out for when they're behaving well and lavish your attention on that.

Providing the child with enough attention is a cornerstone of positive parenting, only if done correctly! Unfortunately, when the child is putting on a tantrum, it's already too late. You have to wait until the emotional storm has passed. Then, when the child has calmed down, you can nurture their need for attention; over time, their tantrums will diminish.

Mistake 2: Resorting to physical punishment

Children are incredibly observant; they notice every habit of their parents and pick up on their behaviors. Just as you can teach your child manners and how to behave well, they can also learn how to misbehave from you. This is because you are your child's role model; they already hold you in a higher position and will look up to you and your behavioral patterns. For example, suppose you notice that your child lashes out and exhibits violent behavior when frustrated or when things don't go their way. In that case, the parent has displayed such aggressive outbursts themselves.

It's a perfect paradigm; if you wish to stop your child from reacting explosively and learn to communicate their feelings rather than lashing out, you must portray the same behavior. Instead of telling your child what to do, it will be more impactful if you actively do those things yourself. When parents resort to violence, which is never acceptable under any circumstances, they do it as a short-cut to achieve discipline and obedience. However, this can cause the child to form dangerous understandings and learn inappropriate behavioral patterns.

Implementing violence causes the child to feel unsafe and angry. They're led to believe that violence is accept-able and can be used if it is "out of love" or to achieve something. They may use violence to gain power over others and abuse their position or come into subordination and not have a mind of their own. Parents make the mistake of using violence, thinking it will "teach" their children a lesson. However, it has the opposite effect; your child loses trust in you and has deep-rooted anger issues.

Using physical methods to teach your child to stop reacting explosively is unreasonable and morally incorrect. Using your hands on your children to teach them to behave is never OK. They will never learn the way that you want them to. While it is difficult for parents to teach good morals and values to children, they can easily set the wrong example. Research suggests that physical discipline is ineffective and harmful and can lead to emotional, behavioral, and academic problems.

Corporal punishment of children does not teach them to identify between right and wrong. Although it may intimidate and scare children to stop their meltdowns, they do not internalize why they should try to do better in the future. What's worse is that they don't even know the better approach to their outbursts; they've never been taught what it is. When around you, your child may behave, but once it's out of sight, it will lead by your example and implement your physical methods on other people.

When faced with conflicts in school or on the playground, your child will resort to physical force, too, because that's how they've seen things happening at home.

Whether they are directly subjected to physical discipline or see or hear it happening around them, they will pick up on it and use it on others to overpower and bully them.

Mistake 3: Embarrassment and humiliation

My father used to pick me up from school every day. He had made it a point to make sure he embarrassed me in front of my friends, whether by asking my friends too many questions, telling personal stories, or using the many "adorable" nicknames he had for me. As a result, I felt embarrassed every day.

Your child feels the same when you embarrass them in public; intentionally or inadvertently, the child will lose faith in the parent. Whether it's for "fun" or trying to shame the child as a tool for shaping their behavior, embarrassing the child publicly does not have any positives but leaves long-lasting adverse effects.

While shaming may seem like working for the time being, shame is a feeling that sticks around and can have a severe and lingering impact on your parent-child relationship and the child's self-esteem. If you attempt to manipulate your child's behavior by revealing personal stories that they trust you with or just knowingly try to make them feel bad about themselves instead of properly communicating about the change you want to see, you are the problem.

Feelings can influence behavior. For example, teaching a child a sense of guilt or regret might motivate them to do better. However, public embarrassment results in the parent losing relational equity and ultimately destroys the child's motivation to improve themselves and work on their behaviors. The correct approach would be to strengthen the bond with your child and lean on that to influence their behavior instead of damaging their self-esteem by publicly embarrassing them.

At this point, it may feel repetitive to keep reading about what you seem to be doing wrong that is stopping your child's behavioral improvement. But without understanding the flaws on your side, you won't be able to teach them to subside their anger, and they will continue to express frustration by lashing out. Parents should reprimand and discipline their children after a meltdown. Trying to reason with a child who lacks the cognitive skill set to express their frustrations effectively will only worsen matters. Parents must commit to remaining in control and staying consistent. It is not an easy task to conquer, and there will be days when you'll slip, and your control over the situation may falter, but you must strive to stay consistent and not lose hope.

Parents are prone to getting anxious about their child's future; they worry whether they'll be able to strive in the real world. They begin to wonder if they're doing a good job and succeeding in getting their own children under control. In times like these, parents have "thinking errors," negative and counterproductive thoughts far from reality. No matter how hard you try, your child's future is in their hands; hence don't force your control over it because if you do, it only worsens for both of you.

Child discipline isn't one size fits all; every child is different, and every child will require a different approach. Just because a particular method worked on one does not mean it will be effective on others. Children have their own quirks and personalities. Hence, as a parent, you must tailor parenting methods to fit those quirks. Parenting is an extremely overwhelming and exhausting job. I repeatedly remind parents to take perpetual breaks to help their mental health and not drain themselves. The temper tantrums can create a negative environment and sometimes feel heavy on the parent's shoulders. Hence, take a break or two; you deserve it!

Children are meant to be playful, noisy, and engage in mischief. On the other hand, parents are told to discipline their children regarding misbehaving. However, to respond with scolding and rebukes to prevent the repetition of mischief – believing that it will benefit the child and allow them to learn their lesson and refrain from behaving like that in the future – is just counterproductive. Parents turn to scolding children because they reason it will be an unpleasant experience for the child, and they will refrain from engaging in that sort of behavior again. In reality, the temptation to misbehave far outweighs the negative experience. Sometimes the child doesn't even remember their previous reprimand, and thus the benefits parents seek from scolding are purely speculative.

Harsh scolding is a traumatic memory that children try to repress because it negatively affects their self-esteem and hurts them greatly, which may provoke them to react more defiantly in the future. Rebuking children in public or private causes them to feel intense shame; experiencing shame in such amounts is unhealthy and creates many forms of emotional disorders, mental illnesses, and addictive behavior later in the child's life. Children tend to believe that they are inherently flawed and that something is "wrong" with them when humiliated- instead of regretful about their actions and wanting to improve.

Constant scolding will leave a lingering impact on your child's life, not just in their childhood but affecting their adult life. They will have developmental problems, unbalanced sleep cycles, difficulties in learning, and an inability to form social relationships. Hence, instead of rebuking the child and making them feel guilty and frustrated, it is critical to treat their mistakes gently and subtly to make them feel safe and supported.

Balanced parenting for balanced children

Parents that become excessively involved in every aspect of their child's life, to the point where they control their academic, athletic, and even social lives, become a hindrance in their child's life and exhibit "Hyper-Parenting," i.e., they take away their liberty to choose how to live and enjoy their lives. In the blind desire to manufacture the perfect and well-rounded child, parents can easily lose themselves and start treating their parenting as competition – all in the race to make the best kid. Crowding children with extracurricular activities – such as music, art and singing lessons, etc. – can leave the child and parent feeling drained. No doubt, individually, these activities are very beneficial. But altogether, children overexert themselves and are left with no creativity to unleash and use their imagination.

Competitive parents will sometimes treat children's lives as a CV for a job at a top company or as a college resume to get into the most elite colleges. Knowing that every decision they make can significantly impact their children's lives, anxiety takes over them. They tend to pressure kids and place huge expectations on their small undeveloped shoulders. Enrolling toddlers in piano classes to make them prodigies is hugely unfair. Forcing children to play competitive sports that they have no clue about is overscheduling them and sometimes more about the parent's desire to have a balanced child than securing a better future.

When parents surround their child with activities and the expectation to excel at each, the child will feel constant scrutiny and will never feel like they are enough if they are only loved and appreciated when they become polished at everything. As a result, children will associate their worth with their excellence at something. This will break their self-esteem and increase their risk of depression, substance abuse, and other defiant behavior. They eventually give up on trying because they've decided that they can never satisfy their parents, so why even bother in the first place.

Developing a balanced child involves more than getting a good percentage or grade on the report card. Instead, it entails growing up resilient, independent, emotionally mature, happy, capable of establishing good relationships, etc. Schools play a crucial role in maturing kids, preparing them for the world, and teaching them how to socialize. However, they still spend most of their time with their parents. It is with the parents that the child's real education begins. Consider children great imitators – they will do as you do and say as you say. Parents form their solid foundation; hence, it is single-handedly their responsibility to provide children with the perfect environment where they will thrive to reach their ultimate potential.

Hence for parents, it is essential to first and foremost take care of themselves. Since children emulate their parents and there's no time they don't act as primary role models, parents must live a healthy and well-balanced lifestyle if they want the children to have the same. Your kids will mirror any lousy parenting skills you exhibit, and they will continue to live by those skills into adulthood. Hence, practicing self-care and creating a positive, healthy environment will rub children the right way and practice it.

Parents should refrain from forcing their children to fit a specific mold instead of appreciating and encouraging their individuality. Not allowing children to think outside the box and stopping them from expressing themselves the way they want can feel oppressive and make them feel insecure about their identity. They'll begin to think that something is wrong with them, and feelings of self-hate will grow. Instead, allow children to openly express their uniqueness, talents, and ideas and not feel ashamed or conditioned to be a certain way.

In addition, parents should encourage children to make decisions that involve challenges and difficulties. While it is understandable to stick to an easy way out when faced with a difficult decision that could result in them facing failure, this will teach kids two lessons in one attempt. One is that they should never shy away from challenges, even if it fails. The second is that failure is a part of life and that it's absurd to think they'll never experience it at some point. Failure should be treated as a teachable moment, allowing the child to grow and learn.

Parents need to realize that their children won't always perform that remarkably. And whether children perform remarkably or not, they will still be appreciated for all the effort they put into the task. A child's efforts should be lauded and encouraged; they need to feel appreciated, understood, and reassured that you believe in them and are confident in their abilities to do better next time.

Children can easily make mistakes; they are perfectly capable of doing that; What matters is owning up to those mistakes, understanding what they did wrong, and apologizing. As parents, you must teach your kids how to say sorry; it is necessary to instill feelings of empathy that will allow them to be seen as more pleasant people to be around and be considered nicer people.

I firmly believe that food brings people together metaphorically to the heart. Hence, I think at least one meal should be eaten together as a family. It fosters healthy communication and results in well-rounded kids that are connected with their families. Engaging in meaningful conversations with your children and asking them about their days makes them feel important and heard – that their opinion is of value. Family dinners allow them to brush up on social skills and improve family bonding.

Allow children to be nothing more and nothing less than children. Don't worry about adult problems; don't discuss such issues with them or even near them. They don't need to stress over bills, marital disputes, etc. Don't place that burden on them because it is not at all theirs to bear.

A household that remains serious and does not encourage a sense of humor feels suffocating for the child. They feel they can't express themselves again and feel unsafe around their parents. On the other hand, it is fun and very relaxing to allow yourself to become a little silly, laugh with your children, and make them feel safe. Children that don't have rigid households have been found to be very easy-going and spontaneous; they enjoy the simpler things in life and try to find joy and positivity no matter what life throws at them.

Lastly, no matter how embarrassed they act later on when they are told they're loved, saying I love you to your children is very important. Even if you think that you show your love and don't need to say it, do it. It doesn't matter; just go for it and make your child happy by expressing how much you love them. Make them feel important and seen, and let them know that their parent's love is unconditional.

So far, we've talked about the making of a defiant and explosive child and how parental mistakes and family background can contribute to it. Avoiding those mistakes is a good step to start interacting with your child freshly and differently, but it is not enough. Explosive children have learned they can get attention and power by being angry, defiant, throwing tantrums, etc. As a result, they've built a habit that takes time and effort to unlearn and replace with healthier behavioral patterns. To perform this transition, parents should strengthen what is already good and gradually diminish misbehavior. This is where the reward system becomes essential. In the next chapter, we'll see how you can modify behaviors by adding pleasant and desirable stimuli or removing aversive stimuli. In this reward system, there is no yelling and no punishment! How is that possible?! You'll find out in the next chapter!

Chapter Three

The Reward System for Behavior Modification

Children need love, especially when they do not deserve it.
Harold Hulbert

In the previous chapters, we discussed the characteristics of an explosive child, the root causes of temper tantrums, what a balanced child is, some typical parenting mistakes, and how to raise a balanced child by avoiding those mistakes. So far, you have learned the potential reasons why your child misbehaves. As mentioned before, parenting starts with you. So, your parenting mistakes is reflected in how your child behaves. Once you correct those mistakes, it is time to use behavior modification techniques to encourage or discourage certain behaviors. The goals are threefold: to gradually create desirable behavioral patterns, weed out undesirable ones, and establish a healthy parent-child relationship.

This chapter will review various reward systems to positively or negatively reinforce behaviors. Rewarding might be the last thing on your mind when your child misbehaves. But believe it or not, positive reinforcement, i.e., rewarding your child's efforts and improvements, works incredibly well for explosive children. Negative reinforcement is equally beneficial when used the right way. First, let's start with a review of positive reinforcement!

What is positive reinforcement?

In simple terms, positive reinforcement encourages good behavior you wish to see more often. It amplifies what is already good and taps into your child's strengths and interests, increasing the odds of responding positively in the future. The idea behind positive reinforcement is that if a favorable reward follows an action, it ensures that the particular behavior occurs again. For example, when parents praise their children for doing their homework, it is more likely that they will complete the homework again to receive the compliments once more. While positive reinforcement can come naturally, saying thank you when your child hands you something you asked for can also be very deliberate. This is when parents want to instill and encourage good behavior and train their children to act a certain way.

Various reward systems for positive reinforcement are suitable for different age groups. So, let's look at the most common types, how to implement each and the effectiveness of these positive reinforcers.

Types of positive reinforcers

You can encourage and praise your child for portraying good behavior in four main ways. Of course, the effectiveness of these various positive reinforcements depends on the individual and the circumstances; Hence, it might be that a particular technique works better or worse than others. Please don't lose hope, and try them all!

Natural reinforcers

If you study day and night, pay attention in class and ask questions, you'll ultimately score well on your tests and get a good grade. Similarly, you'll feel full and energized with a hefty lunch. In both cases, you feel encouraged to repeat the actions since they directly result from the behavior.

Social reinforcers

Social reinforcers are like stamps of approval, mainly in verbal praises or gestures. For example, "You did so well on your test!" or clapping and cheering for them. Physical affection, such as hugs and back taps, are also effective methods. Using such techniques makes children feel loved and appreciated and more inclined toward improving their behavior and doing better.

Tangible reinforcers

Tangible reinforcers are physical, desired objects, such as candy, toys, or even money, as motivation for kids to behave well. For example, giving them a bar of chocolate when they complete their chores or buying them their favorite toy when they get good grades. However, you should not overuse this reinforcement method. Otherwise, your kids will become dependent and behave if they see the prospect of receiving a reward in return. Hence, I would advise using this method sparingly.

Token reinforcers

Children respond best to positive reinforcement expressed creatively. Therefore, engaging them in the process of encouraging improved behavior is an integral step. One such creative and fun method is introducing sticker charts for your young ones and token systems for your older children. The idea of token reinforcers is to establish a form of economy where the kid can exchange a set number of stickers or tokens for a specific reward. For example, you can introduce a system where every completed task earns a token and agree that a certain number of tokens earns them a reward, such as ice cream for dessert after dinner or five more minutes of screen time per token. For this strategy to work, it's vital to set rewards that your kid highly desires.

Examples of Positive Reinforcement

Most parents know about positive reinforcement. However, when it comes to using it, they often end up using it the wrong way or doing it too much or too little. There are many ways you can implement positive reinforcement into your parenting skills. The following examples show how you can practice positive reinforcement with your child.

Verbal Praise

As we discussed earlier, verbally expressing how proud you are of your kid or saying how good they were at a task can do wonders for the child's motivation to do even better in the future. Encouraging them at home or in a public setting by saying "Good job!" with a beaming face is a simple and effective method. Such public acknowledgment will make your child feel proud. In addition, the fact that their parents praised them in front of others will become embedded in their minds, and they will want to repeat the actions that led to that moment. However, as a downside, it can be misconstrued and taken as condescending. Hence, be careful when praising your child; you don't want to overdo it.

Money or presents

For working adults, their positive reinforcement and motivation to wake up early in the morning is money. Kids, especially the older ones, also desire money. Since money can be traded for just about anything; food, toys, and books, the vast number of options excite kids, making them willing to change their behavior and listen to their parents. In addition, they can choose to save money, adopting the habit of saving up and realizing the importance of money early on in life. Presents have a similar role. For example, if your child has managed not to lash out and behave throughout a shopping trip, you can reward their behavior by giving them the liberty to pick a small toy. This shows them that their good behavior is seen and appreciated. Although money or presents are tremendous positive reinforcers, this method can become a heavy burden on your pocket if you rely too often on it. But this is true not only for money but for all forms of reinforcement. In other words, overusing them becomes counterproductive. With money or gifts, the issue becomes tangible soon and fast!

Free Time

As a parent, you should aim to promote a healthy parent-child relationship, which will be difficult to achieve if kids feel that they spend most of their day on homework or completing chores. If your child is non-compliant, I would advise you to offer them free time as an incentive; promise to take them to the park and have lunch there if they finish their tasks and comply. Not only are you positively reinforcing good behavior, you're also encouraging family time and recreation.

Applause

When I have poured my heart and soul into making the most delicious meal for my little one, it can be heartbreaking when they refuse even to take a single bite. Simply scolding them to finish their food won't do any good. So, instead, I have adopted a different approach. I'm sure you've heard of the classic "pretend the spoonful food is an airplane" method; you've probably tried it yourself when your toddler wouldn't eat. Well, I have added to that method – clapping after each bite they take. Applauding at the end of performances isn't unheard of; however, I suggest doing the same for your child. Doing so gives instant results. However, the results aren't long-lasting since there is no physical reward.

Star Charts

Start charts are a creative method of reinforcing positive behavior; you can associate each task with a particular number of stars for further encouragement. For instance, completing homework is five stars, helping with the laundry is two stars, and so on. Doing so encourages collaboration and instills a sense of drive to earn the stars. If you have more than one child, you could also promote a healthy sense of competition between siblings. Star charts usually work very well with younger kids.

Healthy food

While writing this book, I would constantly encourage myself by setting targets before I could have my favorite fruit (watermelon!). By doing so, I used food as an incentive to motivate myself to continue writing. You can adopt the same method for kids; entice them with their favorite food or fruit. For example, tell them, "If you finish cleaning your room quickly, you can have a protein bar" Using food as positive reinforcement has proven successful and influential – who would say no to delicious food anyways? The problem is that most kids like unhealthy food, such as cookies or candy.

Nevertheless, they probably like other healthier food like milk, protein bars, fruits, flavored yogurt, or dried fruits. Therefore, try to offer them two or three types of healthy food for their good behavior. In addition, giving them the possibility to make their own choice will enhance the likelihood of sticking with healthy food as a positive reinforcer. Children seek power, and letting them make choices is a great way to fulfill this need!

Reading about these different examples of implementing positive reinforcement has enabled you to use this strategy the right way. This method can help promote good behavior that you want to see more of, and positive reinforcement can also work for angry kids. So, if you want to know how to use positive reinforcement to deal with explosive kids, keep reading!

How does positive reinforcement work for angry kids?

Now that you know more about positive reinforcement, let's see how we can use it for difficult, explosive kids. Anger is a common emotion felt by everyone, and that includes children as well. Just as you'd find it normal for an adult to lose their composure and lash out when they get frustrated and find no words to express themselves, a child's explosive behavior shouldn't come as a surprise either. With their limited vocabulary, it's understandable that they'd use their anger as a form of expression. You, as a parent, should realize that their lashing out is an attempt at communication; rather than a reflection of your parenting skills. Once you've understood this, learning about effective methods to deal with angry kids becomes easier.

One such method is reinforcing positive reinforcement – hailed as one of the most effective methods to encourage positive changes in demeanor, and modify behavior to prevent negative behavior. Unfortunately, the concept of doing good things without getting any appreciation is difficult to instill in kids. It would be great if children could do good without the intention of getting praised. However, in the beginning, you can't expect your child to practice good behavior if they don't receive positive reinforcement. Just as you wouldn't go to work without the incentive of getting paid, kids also need a push in the right direction, be motivated, and be encouraged to exhibit good behavior.

But how does positive reinforcement help when your child reacts explosively and is unwilling to listen and cooperate? You'll fail if you try to reason with your child when they're already struggling to express their frustrations. On the other hand, if you respond to the angry child with the same intensity, you will only teach them that anger and yelling is an acceptable way to communicate their feelings. Instead, you ought to understand what sets your child off. Learn what your kids' triggers are and work together to try to prevent future outbursts. As a parent, you should look for patterns and see what upsets your child, what happens before, or how they feel before lashing out. If going to school early in the morning angers your kid, attempt to verbalize feelings with them and teach them to use words instead of letting their emotions get a hold of them.

Once you've identified what upsets them, learned what precedes their outbursts, and worked together to practice using words as a form of expression, you can practice positive reinforcement with them. Encourage them when they choose the right outlets to express themselves instead of just resorting to screaming and behaving explosively. For example, praising your child for telling you why they dislike going to school is more effective than telling them that they have no other choice and have to go. Kids find it difficult to handle their anger calmly; they find it confusing and frustrating that they aren't able just to say how and why they feel a certain way. So, be patient with them and appreciate their efforts. For instance, if your child is being unreasonable and not sharing during playtime with their friends or siblings, treat them gently and remind them to express how they feel. Then, after they've calmed down, appreciate them for being able to calm down and praise them for trying to vent their frustrations verbally – at least they're trying. Hence, rewarding behavior you want to see more often is more important than solely focusing on what your child did wrong.

Positive vs. Negative Reinforcement

In 1938, B.F. Skinner developed the concept of "Operant Conditioning" to explain complex human behaviors and how rewards and consequences determine the probability of a behavior being repeated. Reinforcement is a significant concept in Operant Conditioning, which can be further sub-categorized into positive and negative reinforcement.

When it comes to Operant Conditioning, negative and positive have different meanings than how you'd usually use them. In Operant Conditioning, positive means adding a pleasant and desirable stimulus. On the other hand, negative reinforcement is removing an aversive stimulus. So, "positive" or "negative" does not refer to the quality of the reinforcers. Instead, both reinforcers reward the operant, i.e., the person who exhibits a specific behavior. Positive reinforcement increases the frequency and probability of desired behaviors by adding an external and pleasant stimulus after exhibiting that behavior. In the case of negative reinforcement, the goal is to suppress behavior by removing an external but unpleasant stimulus once that behavior is stopped.

You use a positive reinforcer when you reward your child with a piece of cake when they clean their room. Our everyday life is rich with rewards for desirable actions. Without such rewards, we wouldn't function as a society. For instance, getting good grades is a reward for students that have studied hard. At the same time, you may argue that students should work hard and not slack; the positive reinforcement they receive from getting accepted into the colleges of their dreams increases their odds of continuing to work hard.

Suppose you present your child with the desired stimulus right after they exhibit a desirable behavior in the form of food or toys. In that case, you're increasing the likelihood of them showing the same behavior in the future. Likewise, praising your kid when they start doing their homework without you telling them to will encourage and motivate them to complete their school work independently.

Negative reinforcement is the reinforcement of the desired behavior by removing an aversive stimulus. For example, the constant beeping sound you hear when you sit in your car and don't wear a seat belt is an excellent – and annoying instance of negative reinforcement. If something pleasant replaces the triggering beeping sound, the odds of you fastening your seatbelt in the future will decrease drastically. You can implement this strategy with children as well. For instance, kids can be picky regarding foods – especially healthy ones, such as broccoli. Getting them to finish their food can become a hefty task, so what are you to do? You could encourage them by telling them they can excuse themselves from the table once they've finished. Doing so removes the aversive stimulus (sitting at the dinner table) once the desired behavior is exhibited (finishing their food). This will increase the probability of your child finishing their food in the future.

Differences and similarities between positive and negative reinforcement

While positive reinforcement is the concept of presenting desirable stimuli to increase the odds of specific behavior, negative reinforcement involves giving such reinforcers that the operant (for example, your kid!) will want to avoid. Negative reinforcers are undesirable and aversive. The motivation to keep doing a particular behavior comes from the desire to prevent these reinforcers. This contrasts with positive reinforcement, which encourages subjects with desirable stimuli.

You can practice positive reinforcement at home by introducing a favorable stimulus; for instance, a good report card earns a new toy. This will encourage your child to work hard to get their favorite toy. Similarly, you could introduce a less favorable stimulus and motivate your child to exhibit certain behaviors if they want to avoid the unpleasant reinforcer. For example, increasing the chores they must complete if they become defiant will make them more likely to comply to avoid doing any extra duties.

Although positive and negative reinforcers use entirely different reward mechanisms, they have the same end goal of behavioral modification. So in that sense, they are very similar. In both cases, the primary purpose is to increase the probability and frequency of a behavior. In addition, the success rate of both positive and negative reinforcement is proportional to how consistently and frequently you respond to the subject's behavior.

The right way to positively reinforce

As mentioned earlier, most parents are aware of the concept of positive reinforcement; However, they often lack the implementation skills. In other words, while they understand what positive reinforcement is and what it entails, practically enforcing it can be challenging for many. There are various strategies you can use to hone your reinforcement skills. Here are the primary ones:

Associate rewards to behaviors

Sometimes children need that little push; they need to understand that their good behaviors don't go unnoticed; you should show your child that good things happen when they exhibit positive behavior. And you can do that by linking the rewards you offer to the particular behavior you wish to reinforce. For instance, if your child tidies up their play area without you nagging them, you can let them stay up for a while so they can play for longer. Or, if your child helps you prepare dinner, you can let them choose what to have for dessert. In each case, you're forming a bridge between the behavior you want to see more often and the reward. Again, this method is proven effective as it creates a memory in children's minds associating positive behavior with a good outcome.

If your kid is consistently and frequently exhibiting the desired behavior, you can even give them the liberty to choose what they would want as their reward. While giving a child such autonomy may sound illogical, this approach instills a feeling of control in the child. In addition, by allowing them to choose their reward, you're giving them another source of motivation to improve themselves and do better in the future.

Avoid accidental positive reinforcement

When your child is disobedient, non-compliant, and misbehaving, any amount of attention you give them is bad. Whether you're scolding or trying to reason with them doesn't matter. Instead of ignoring them when they're like this, giving them attention will only reinforce their behavior.

If your child is refusing to do anything you say, don't react by saying, "Listen to me!" or "Behave yourself!". If you indulge in their antics like this, they'll feel reinforced to continue to act this way. Parents tend to reinforce negative behavior unintentionally. In their eyes, they're only trying to discipline and teach their child to behave. However, this can backfire badly. If you give in to your child's negative behavior, they'll learn to use that against you and try to gain control of matters. For example, if your child is having a breakdown at the supermarket, begging and whining to get a pricey toy, they will continue to do so until and unless you give in. If you give in, the kid's nasty and improper behavior is validated, and they'll get encouraged to behave the same way when they want something in the future.

Instead of giving your defiant child the time of day, or giving in to their demands, ignore them and make sure to discourage such behavior instead of reinforcing it. Instead, present them with a negative consequence, such as reduced screen time or no dessert after dinner, and remain determined to follow through with it.

Be consistent

"Consistency is key" I'm sure you've heard of this many times, on many different occasions, whether you're working out or studying (or even baking). If you're not practicing something consistently, it won't yield results.

The more often you do something, the better results you will yield. It is the same with positive reinforcement; if you reward your kids' positive behavior consistently, you will begin to see massive improvements in their behavior. Parents usually make the mistake of offering big rewards every time for comparatively less demanding tasks. For example, treating your child to a new toy every time they clean their room will promote unhealthy and unrealistic standards. It will result in your child believing that they should only follow what you say if it has something in it for them.

Younger children need a little extra push and motivation to practice good behavior. Hence the more you praise them for their efforts, the better. It can be scary for your little one to learn a new behavior or practice a specific skill. At times like that, it's up to you to encourage them by offering positive reinforcement consistently. To bring some consistency, you can implement the sticker system previously mentioned. That way, you won't have to provide physical rewards for every good behavior. Instead, engage your child by offering them a sticker every time they exhibit specific behavior. For instance, you can praise them and offer a sticker in return every time they put their toys away after a playing session. You could also establish a currency system to motivate your child further, setting up bigger rewards for a specific number of stickers. If you stray away from offering positive reinforcement every time your little one portrays a specific behavior, they will get demotivated and fail to understand why they should behave well in the first place. Hence, adopting a more consistent, rewarding routine is imperative, especially for younger children.

Make the Reinforcement Immediate

Suppose your child misbehaved last week; they didn't listen to you when you asked them to help you out with the cleaning and instead talked back to you. But today, they helped you make dinner without having to ask. If you hold that poor behavior over their heads and refrain from giving your child the praise they deserve, they will ultimately lose motivation and stop trying. Instead, the strategy that you should approach is implementing positive reinforcement as soon as the good behavior occurs. Doing so creates a consistent environment where your child feels confident and encouraged to follow what you say.

Set attainable expectations

It's unfair to set unattainable expectations for your child; doing so will only demoralize them to the point where they won't even want to try. If your targets are not within their reach, they'll fail to see the point in behaving well and have no motivation to do better. For example, if you expect your child to help you set up the table for dinner, complete all their chores, and do their homework on time, you are expecting far too much from a child in the first place. Instead of rewarding only based on accomplished tasks, reward improvements and efforts. For example, if your child began working on their homework without you asking them but got distracted while doing it, you should praise them for starting in the first place.

What isn't advised is setting up parallels between siblings and using a child as a benchmark for the others. While you may have good intentions, it will only create animosity between siblings. If they realize their efforts aren't as praised as their siblings, they'll eventually lose motivation to try.

The wrong way to positively reinforce

If you have previously tried reinforcement techniques and have not received your desired results, it may be because you have made common mistakes in your reinforcement strategies. For example, the following are three mistakes parents make when implementing positive reinforcement:

Assuming you know what motivates your child

As a parent, you may think that you know everything about your child; what they like, what they don't like, and what they need or don't need. Well, I am sorry, but that may not always be accurate. For example, you may assume that your youngest would love stickers and candies while her older brothers would prefer a sleepover. What if you are proven wrong?! Regarding younger children, toys and sweets are effective. However, they soon grow out of them and want new and different things. If you keep offering to get them a toy from the series they liked a while back, and they still don't feel motivated, it's probably because they've outgrown that series and now have different interests. To counter this, give them many choices (not too many, though, as that will only confuse them). This will give them the liberty to choose, feel more in control, and be encouraged. So, please pay attention to what your kid feels most excited about and their changing preferences over time.

When it comes to older children, things get a little trickier. You would think they would gravitate towards trips with friends or having their friends over for a party. However, that may not hold for everyone. I remember that while I did not care for having friends over, I would have done right about anything to be able to play the piano. But how are parents supposed to know what interests their kids over time? The answer is to establish a strong relationship with your older children, connect with them and get to know the quirky interest they want to pursue or talk about. Even listening to what they like nowadays and find attractive can encourage them as they will feel validated and safe.

Neglecting to bond with your child

Parents forget that if they mindlessly keep rewarding children with material things, they'll soon have to meet ever-increasing demands from their kids. With time, interests change, and the things that once motivated your child won't have the same effect now. For example, your child may want to learn to play the piano today. However, with time they might become more interested and improve their skills to the point where they will want to have a piano at home. Such demands may not be reasonable for many parents, so what are you to do? When faced with such unreasonable demands, a healthy, positive relationship with your child comes in handy. I understand that, at times, our interests and passions can be entirely different from our children's. However, if you try to relate to your kids' niches and take an interest in them, it will make them want to listen to you. Everyone wants someone they can relate to and can share a common interest with; everyone wants to talk to someone that would be willing to listen and find their passions interesting. If you and your child share a relationship that promotes a healthy bond of communication and interests, they won't feel the need to make high demands to feel motivated.

If your kid is interested in a particular genre of music, try listening to that genre to understand your kid's likes. When dropping them off at school, you can listen to the same music and bond over it. Ask your child questions about their areas of interest; make them want to come and talk to you about what has piqued their interest lately. By doing so, your time spent with your child is spent wisely, and they can share what they love with you. Building up your relationship with your child can give you the ability to get them to listen to you and be compliant. You can use this bond as a reinforcer and get them to exhibit good behaviors. For instance, ask your child to set the table while they tell you about the latest music they're into.

Not only can you reinforce positive behavior, but you can also share ideas with your child and make it a collaborative effort. While they may get bored of particular interests, you can develop different and engaging activities to strengthen the positive bond between parent and child. While the parent is the one with control in the dynamic, if you make the child feel more welcome and treat them as if you are their friend, they'll feel more comfortable with and capable of responding to your demands. If you make your child feel like they're special, then it will help them see it too.

Positive reinforcement is not just about food.

You may reach for your kid's snack when they oblige to your demands, behave themselves, and exhibit behaviors you want to see more often in the future. Likewise, you may use unhealthy food as an incentive to encourage them to exhibit certain behaviors or to reward them for doing a good job. Again, this is a legitimate technique and can work wonderfully to enforce positive reinforcement. Similarly, you may even withhold their favorite treats as a punishment for bad behavior. For example, suppose your child talked back or refused to clean their room; you could respond by not letting them have ice cream as dessert after dinner. Both are great strategies to encourage good behavior from your kid in the future. However, they can soon affect your child's eating habits if not executed properly.

Positive reinforcement is not all about food. Hence, if you often reward your child's good behavior with sweets, chips, or other junk food high in sugar, calories, and fat, it can ultimately lead to overeating and obesity. For example, if they get their favorite candy every time they clean their room, it will interfere with their natural ability to regulate their food intake. In addition, it will encourage them to exhibit good behavior for the wrong reasons; if they understand that their favorite candy awaits them, they'll be obedient just to reward themselves even when they're not hungry.

Offering foods with little nutritional value as a reward for good behavior can confuse children. As parents, we try to teach healthy eating habits and tell kids to avoid foods high in sugar and fat. So, it can send a mixed message if you start rewarding good behavior with the same foods you keep off-limits. But on the other hand, allowing your child to indulge in unhealthy foods to behave well can result in them associating junk foods with certain moods; they'll begin to think that it's OK to indulge in sweets when they feel good about themselves. For example, if you offer a piece of chocolate for every chore your child completes, they will be motivated to do more chores without complaining, but at what cost? Since you turn to sweets as a reward for "good" behavior, they become more appealing to your child than healthier options.

On the other hand, if you opt for using food as a punishment for bad behavior, forcing your child to finish what's on their plate can encourage them negatively. Your child will be encouraged to form bad eating habits, such as eating despite feeling full. Also, since they're being forced to eat, they'll develop a distaste for nutritious foods.

Instead of using foods as a reinforcer, there are many other strategic methods to reinforce good behavior positively. For example, by telling them you'll take them to the zoo, planetarium, or any other place they want to visit. If your child has artistic skills and interests, you could also give them the incentive to buy art supplies, canvases, or coloring books. As a kid, I would love to buy new stationery for school. Similarly, I'm sure your little one also looks forward to buying school supplies. So, you can offer to take them on stationery shopping as a reward for good behavior instead of using food. You can also try to incorporate more family time into the child's routine, whether playing their favorite game with them or listening to music together. By doing so, you're encouraging a healthy parent-child relationship.

Do not mix negative reinforcement and punishment!

Just like positive reinforcement, correct execution is vital for negative reinforcement to work. Unfortunately, many parents mix up negative reinforcement with punishment. While they intend to reinforce a behavior negatively, they end up punishing their child and miss the reinforcement aspect altogether. Punishment is similar to reinforcement; since it could include adding or removing a stimulus. The key here is to understand that reinforcement, whether positive or negative, is to strengthen a behavior.

In contrast, punishment is to weaken a particular behavior. So, for example, a teacher can eliminate the homework if students work hard in class and get good grades (negative reinforcement by removing an undesirable stimulus, i.e., the homework). But on the other hand, the teacher can also give more homework if the students get poor grades (positive punishment by adding an undesirable stimulus, i.e., more homework). So, remember that reinforcement is to strengthen good behavior and is fundamentally different than punishment.

Reinforcing your desired behaviors positively or negatively could work fabulously. But not if you do not practice what you preach! Your children are always watching and modeling your behavior, how you handle stress, how you treat others, whether you keep your promises, etc. Remember, parenting starts with you! You are a role model for your children, especially younger ones. The next chapter discusses how you could be a positive role model and lay a solid behavioral foundation for your beloved children by becoming a better version of yourself! Curious? Just keep reading!

Chapter Four

The Imitation Game

Children have never been very good at listening to their elders, but they have never failed to imitate them.
James Baldwin

Most parents feel frustrated when they repeatedly tell their children what to do and how to behave. But "for some reason," they continue to act out and not comply. You, too, might have felt hopeless at one point, feeling exhausted by telling them to behave repeatedly but to no avail. To all the parents that believe they can change their child's attitude for the better by just saying what they should do, I hate to break it to you, but your efforts will never bear fruits. 80% of your learning comes from visual knowledge. Hence, your kid's primary character development and understanding come from the environment they're present in; they will do what they see, not what they hear!

Our brains are developed so that we are more capable of processing images than we are of processing words. That is why you're more inclined to imitate what you see than to comply with what you are told to do. As adults, we've often used the phrase, "Actions speak louder than words," when talking about relationships and how ingenuine it seems when actions don't accompany words. Well, the exact theory applies to children. You can spend the entire day telling your child about the harsh realities of the world; you can attempt to teach them appropriate reactions to complex emotions with words, and you may even try to instill good morals by lecturing them. But all this will essentially go in vain if you do not back up your words with your actions.

Children are already curious and confused creatures, they're brought into a strange world where they're expected to navigate its complexities. On that note, expecting them to understand and follow what you tell them to do is unfair. While I know that words are crucial in some situations and needed to communicate and reach your child, using words without backing them up with actions is like pouring into a broken vessel. For instance, if you lash out and lose composure when things get overwhelming, your child will learn that and exhibit the same behavior when they feel angry or overwhelmed. No matter how much you tell them they should use their words to express frustrations, they won't because they've never seen you do it yourself.

Similarly, if your child is having a breakdown and crying, and you raise your voice at them and tell them to calm down, you're only making matters worse. Doing so sends mixed signals by not practicing what you preach and calming yourself down before dealing with your explosive child. On the other hand, if you yell at your child to behave when they're misbehaving, you're unintentionally teaching them that they can get their point across by raising their voice. As the saying goes, "Watch and learn", your kids do that and pick up on your habits and reactions to situations. Hence, it doesn't matter how much you tell your child to do something or how well you can get your point across with words because your child will do as you do and not as you say.

Being a model for your Kid

How do our children look up to us so much that they try to emulate our actions and beliefs? Let's review some aspects of your child's life that directly reflect how they see you. We've already established that the parent is the first role model of their child, the primary source of character development, and the means of instilling good morals and beliefs. Therefore, how you behave around your child determines how your child will behave around others. Hence, you are responsible for visually showing your child all the behaviors you want to see in them. Otherwise, their ability to take charge of their lives and manage emotions will suffer.

If you want to make your child responsible and honest but are confused about why you aren't making progress with them, try exhibiting those behaviors yourself first. How often you tell your child to speak the truth doesn't matter. If you fail to live out your practices and implement the very things you say, your children will never learn. If you lie about your kid's age to get into places for free, it'll signal that lying is acceptable if you get something in return. Hence, you can't blame your child since they're just doing as they see at home.

Once you become a parent, you will always have a very attentive audience eager to imitate your actions. So, be careful of what you say and do around your kids because they will soak in every piece of information. For example, suppose you pass negative comments behind people's backs and/or use demeaning language around your children. In that case, you should prepare yourself to be embarrassed by your child repeating them afterward, probably at the wrong times. On the other hand, if you portray a negative attitude despite what you say, your children will pick on your physical deeds and mimic them. The good news is that this goes both ways. If you exhibit good behaviors and display good habits, your children will learn more than they ever will from your words.

As parents, we want our children to be loving and easy-going. But how can you expect that to happen when you don't provide your child with a caring and easy-going environment? Kids flourish if they are present in an environment where their needs are met and don't feel stifled. If you want your child to treat others in life with love and respect, you must treat them – and others around them– with that love and respect first. For example, suppose you establish a calm and healthy environment at home where frustrations are dealt with patience and understanding and not by lashing out. In that case, you are teaching your children that reacting explosively to frustrations isn't the way to cope with them. On the other hand, it'll become difficult to train them to use their words when you lose your calm when faced with difficulties. Hence, while I understand how exhausting and difficult it can be, try to become a pillar of patience for your child and lead by example to teach them that this is how you should lead with the ups and downs of life.

As a parent, you're supposed to fill in the role of a positive role model and become the ideal "mirror" that your children's lives will reflect. However, to become that, you first need to familiarize yourself with the imitation game kids partake in and understand how their development is interlinked.

The mirror effect

Who doesn't like an excellent spot-on imitation? I find it admirable how people can mimic other people's quirks so well. However, you may not see your child's mimicry of you as enjoyable unless you're a great and positive role model, so you have nothing to worry about. You are your child's first teacher, and since they spend most of their day with you, they observe and watch all your moves and listen in on everything you say. Creepy, I know! The innate trait to copy the parent's actions and words can begin as early as 18 months. An adorable and humorous example is when your barely one-year-old picks up a phone and holds it to their ear. While they do not understand what they are doing, it seems reasonable because their mother or father does it. But why does your one-year-old like to pick up the cell phone in the first place? Why do children imitate parents at all? While it may seem like a relatively simple question, it has many different answers.

Anatole France (the French poet, journalist, and novelist who died in 1924) was spot-on when he said, "The greatest virtue of man is perhaps curiosity." Children are brought into a strange and new world with zero understanding and experience of how it works and must discover things independently. Thus, it's safe to say that your child feels more curious about learning the ways of the world than you are. This drive causes them to mimic whatever they see happening around them. Since guardians spend the most time around the kid, their influence is the greatest. A child's desire to learn more about their environment and its people is one of the reasons behind your child's mimicry of you.

Imagine yourself in a foreign land with strange people that speak an alien language. You would perhaps feel puzzled and frustrated at your inability to connect or familiarize yourself with the environment; similar is the case with very young children. They cannot communicate with us, do not understand their feelings, and are not mentally developed enough to address and accept their emotions. Instead, they rely on the environment to provide that base understanding. Since kids don't know any better and copy what they've seen growing up, it explains why children brought up in households with a history of violence are violent. In contrast, children reared in loving and accepting families are more compassionate and calmer.

Imitation is necessary for your child's development; they can learn different skills quickly and efficiently through visual aid. There are plenty of other benefits to mimicry between Child and parent. Here are some examples:

Bonding

When I mentioned the creepiness of your child imitating everything you say and do, I forgot how adorable and endearing it is to see them putting themselves in your shoes. Seeing your kid copying your mannerisms and unexpectedly repeating things you've said can invoke a stronger bond between you and your little one.

Your child imitating you can sometimes feel exhilarating, knowing someone is looking up to you and mimicking your ways. You can't help but feel a more robust and healthier bond growing.

Independence

As parents, we strive to instill independence in our kids so that they don't feel the need to come to us for every little thing. Many parents struggle with making their children less dependent on them. Your child's innate feature to imitate will help you in this case. For example, Suppose you are someone that does not know how to cook and typically isn't found in the kitchen. In that case, you should occasionally try to cook something. By doing so, show your child that they should be willing to step up and try to do things independently, even if they don't excel. If you do things independently, your child will try to imitate that. Once they do, they'll feel a surge of power in their ability to do something, just like their parents.

Language development

We take such joy in our child's first words, to the point where we make it a cause for celebration. However, there wouldn't be anything to celebrate if it weren't for your child's ability to imitate what you say to them or others around them. A child's language development heavily depends on the parent's speech. Hence, always try to use a softer and kinder tone when with kids or around them so they can adopt a similar manner. Due to the importance of mimicry in language development, I highly recommend reading to your child so they can hear the words and someday say them back to you. However, while it can be a delight to listen your child repeat your words and tone, it can also be embarrassing if they pick up on some curse words!

Good morals

If your child hears you use demeaning language for a particular ethnic or religious group, they will begin to have the same prejudices. Whether being discriminatory towards characters on a TV show or biased over certain cultures, your little one will pick on them and become just as inequitable. But, on the other hand, if you speak to your child and other people around your child with fairness, they'll begin to be just as fair and grow up to become upstanding individuals in society.

Angry parents, angry kids

If children are such great copycats, what happens when they see angry, disappointed, or messed up parents? Numerous studies have found that parents that tend to get angry quickly and go off the rails are more likely to have children that exhibit violent behaviors and have more frequent temper tantrums. Again, this is because children mirror their parents' words and actions. We can call this the "Mirror Effect". Once you become a parent, many of your daily experiences become mutual. Your child observes your actions and reactions and reflects them on you like a mirror. Children have an eye for your emotional shifts and try to mimic them, and since they cannot express their feelings well, they look to you for ways to express themselves. Hence, if you're expressing your frustration by lashing out or choosing to yell and become distant when faced with difficulties, chances are so will your kid.

This mirroring between you and your child can be a challenge at times. It can seem like you don't have any privacy to react as you wish without it coming to haunt you in the form of imitation by your kid. Although it is not easy to keep calm when your kid throws a hissy fit over the smallest of things, if you don't manage your anger in heated moments like these, you're only teaching your child to do the same. In moments like these, when your patience is being tested, you need anger management more than ever. Imagine you are trying to enjoy some peace in the lounge, but you hear your children fighting over a toy. You try your best to ignore the voices hoping they'll figure it out independently. But to your dismay, you hear doors slamming, screams and cries. The anger starts boiling inside you. What do you do now? Do you rush into the room and yell at them to behave themselves? Doing that will teach your children that they can raise their voices when feeling angry. Imagine the alternative; you walk into the room calmly and address the situation without lashing out. Your anger will subside, and you managed to be a good role model!

Modeling and Teaching Calm down Behaviors

Parents regularly face daily situations when their kids throw tantrums, do not comply, or behave explosively. What can you do to handle such situations well and simultaneously provide a good learning moment for your kids? As the starting point, always think of the behavior patterns you want to see more in your child and the ones you hope to see less often. Your goal is to amplify the former and diminish the latter. Here are some guidelines for handling challenging: moments:

Taking a time-out

Never attempt to resolve a tantrum when emotions are high. Reacting harshly during a wild temper tantrum is usually counterproductive. Instead, take some time to calm down until you feel composed and ready to talk with your kid about their explosive meltdown. For example, if your child is breaking down over not wanting to eat their food, step away from the room and tell them that you'll be taking a time-out until you feel calm enough to address the situation without lashing out. You can even designate a particular part of the house as a "chill spot" where you go to calm down. Decorate this spot with fun and engaging activities like books, puzzles, or videos to make it feel more welcoming. Don't just reserve the area for yourself. Instead, make it a practice at home for everyone to head towards the "chill spot" when feeling stressed or frustrated.

Counting to calm anger

When angry, parents can say pretty harsh things that they don't mean but can continue to affect the children. Hence, this method will help you not say anything hurtful to your kid that will affect them for a lifetime. The method's purpose is to slowly count to ten or twenty before responding angrily to your already sensitive child. During explosive tantrums, it's better to tell them you're going to count to ten instead of responding to the frustrating situation immediately. Of course, it would help if you encouraged your kid to do it with you.

Taking some deep breaths

It sounds like a cliché. But believe it or not, taking deep breaths quickly leads your mind and body to a calmer state. You may not realize it, but your body adopts a different breathing style when upset. You take shallow breaths that keep you agitated. Being intentional and taking slower and deeper breaths can calm your mind and body. Since the mind and body are interconnected, you need to first calm down your body by taking deliberate deep breaths, and once you do that, your mind won't be far back in achieving that calm state either. Deep breathing is often the easiest method to gain better control over your emotions so that you do not take them out on your children.

Becoming a role model your child deserves

So far, we have discussed why children imitate their parents, including their wrong behaviors, and explained some techniques to keep those behaviors in check. However, I've yet to provide you with ways you can prove to be an excellent role model for your little one. Since this chapter would be incomplete without it, let's dig into some ways you can be a good role model. Remember to lead by example for your child and emulate all the healthy habits and good behavior you want to instill in your child. How can you do that? Here are a few tips:

Start early

"The earlier, the better." It will bode well for you if you adopt this motto regarding inculcating good habits in children. Even if your kid can't form words yet, they're still very impressionable; and while they may not understand it, they will focus on how they feel and attempt to imitate that feeling. Since you cannot become a good role model overnight, starting early by taking baby steps in the right direction is better.

Taking care of yourself

Once you become a parent, you find it difficult to focus on yourself and care for yourself and your needs. However, if you prioritize your health and do what makes you happy, your children will follow and learn how important it is to do things that make them happy. Your little one – seeing you do something for yourself, such as reading or relaxing by going out with your friends-will want to mimic the joy of doing things for yourself. By doing so, you're teaching the understanding that it's essential to set time aside for yourself and do things that bring them joy. Being a role model is like putting airplane masks on. First, put your mask on before helping others!

Being positive

Optimism is an important concept to understand; however a rather difficult one. You need to express positivity in difficult times, but not so much that they become unrealistic and form delusions. As a parent, you should teach your child not to lose hope and keep their head high when any trouble befalls them. Your child needs to understand that difficulties are a part of life that you must take as a challenge and beat.

Setting goals

As a parent, you want your child to do well in school, be motivated, and have a sense of discipline to achieve things. But how do you expect them to have that if you don't model that behavior yourself? Setting goals for yourself, like waking up early and taking a morning jog, requires discipline and organizing. It requires a great deal of motivation to stick to a goal. But if you do, your little one will see you working hard towards your goals and, in turn, understand the importance of having a sense of direction. Whether it's a small goal like cleaning the playroom or a big one like studying hard for a test, help your children set their own goals and encourage them to work towards them.

The main takeaway of this chapter is that you are the role model for your child, so try to be a good one! What happens if you aren't? What if you yell instead of communicating? The next chapter is about removing yelling from your parenting toolbox. You might wonder what new tools you can use as a replacement. There is a wide range of them, and we'll discuss them in detail!

Chapter Five

Protecting Your Vocal Cords!

Children are educated by what the grown-up is and not by his talk.

Carl Jung

Yelling is still a widespread parenting tool, unfortunately! According to a 2003 study published in the Journal of Marriage and Family, more than 90 percent of the parents surveyed (a sample of 991 parents) reported using one or more forms of psychological aggression, such as angry shouting, cursing, calling a child a dummy, etc. By child age of five, the number was 98 percent! This data shows that acts of psychological aggression (mainly yelling) are a near-universal disciplinary tactic of American parents. To make matters worse, yelling does not help and even creates more behavioral issues. For example, a 2013 study conducted by the University of Pittsburgh's School of Education and psychology shows that the use of harsh verbal discipline, in fact, aggravates problematic behaviors in adolescents.

A child's misbehaviors and defiance, combined with various parenting stresses, create the perfect storm to push the parents over their limits. We're all guilty of yelling at our kids, and I am sure most of us regret that. So, how can we go toward yell-free parenting? This chapter is to aid parents who want to connect with their explosive children, understand their feelings, and eliminate the yelling. First, we'll review how yelling affects children and then discuss a toolbox to help you stop exercising your vocal cords too much while parenting your child!

Yelling at Kids: Not Recommended!

No one likes getting yelled at, whether adults at the workplace or little children at home or school. Getting yelled at doesn't make the message clearer nor encourage us to listen to the one yelling at us. Instead, it instills fear and anxiety. Similarly, if you're yelling at your child to discipline them, you only make them feel insecure and embarrassed. Recent studies have concluded that yelling can result in more aggressive behavior in children. Hence, while you may think that your yelling will improve your kids' behavior, the reality is that it does not help at all.

Feeling angered by a defiant attitude is reasonable. However, expressing that anger by screaming and yelling is counterproductive and very harmful. How harmful, you may ask? Well, let's discuss that.

Kids cannot learn in "fight-or-flight mode."

The fight-or-flight response is our brain telling us that we're in a threatening situation and, as the name suggests, must either fight the matter or flee. You may have noticed this in how your child responds to getting yelled at; they may retaliate physically, run away from you, or even stay stuck in one place to avoid unnecessary attention. When you're relieving your anger by yelling at them, your child doesn't see the matter as a learning opportunity since the part of their brain that deals with learning shuts down in threatening situations. So, all your yelling does not give you any benefits. It only makes you look like the bad guy in your child's eyes; they will begin viewing you as a threat and will eventually attempt to stay away from you to protect themselves. As a parent, you do not want to take up the role of the villain in your kid's movie. You do not want to place them in a situation where they must fear and comply because they are afraid of the consequences. Growing up in a household where yelling and screaming are the ways to express anger and frustration results in children behaving the same way with others when they are older.

Yellers model poor communication skills.

If you are a parent that has adopted yelling as a disciplinary method, you must've noticed your child's response to this technique. Toddlers may cry, while older children tend to shut down and become distant. In either case, you are not reaching your kid, and instead, they're learning to detach from all the parental connections they may have with you. Your kid depends on you to teach them how to express and feel their emotions and frustration. If you fail to provide an environment where they feel comfortable and safe talking about their feelings, they will become distant and lack essential communication skills. If you fly off the handle at every inconvenience, you teach your child to respond similarly to situations. Hence, once they have grown up and encountered an unpleasant scenario, they will scream and yell just as you did or still do. In short, if you keep yelling at your child, you should prepare for a lifetime of yelling battles.

Your yell-free parenting toolbox

Regardless of how explosive children may behave to shift control to themselves, the guardian-child dynamic places the guardian in a position of control and power. Hence, the guardian figure must take up healthier methods to express their anger and prevent a communication gap between them and the child. Studies suggest that parents who yell at their kids to express their anger and disappointment cause them to be more prone to anxiety and higher levels of depression..Imagine you're being taken care of by someone more than twice your size, and this creature feeds you, provides you with all the essentials, and even plays around with you. Now consider how terrified you would be if this mega-sized guardian started screaming and yelling at you! On that note, it's only reasonable to conclude that a child in that situation would feel terrified and lose the sense of security that parents provide.

Parenthood can be overwhelming when you have to deal with household chores, workplace responsibilities, and a child with little understanding of their feelings. So what does one do in such situations? How does a parent discipline their child when acting up and being defiant? What parenting approach should they adopt that does not harm their child or themselves? Every child is different, and it would be unrealistic to provide surefire techniques. However, we can always think of some general guidelines as the starting point to discipline your angry kid without making them insecure. You can use take the following tips and tailor them to suit your situation:

Recognize and reinforce positive behaviors.

Since children view parents as role models, it's understandable that they want to behave well to receive praise and acceptance from their parents. And if they get the approval and recognition they seek, they will want to repeat their actions to make them more frequent. A tone like "Thank you for using words and telling me what was bothering you instead of just crying and wailing."

praises good behavior and makes them feel appreciated, encourages the child not to throw a tantrum, and communicates with the parent. Yelling has the opposite effect. Research suggests that if you yell or scream at your child, you have to praise them five times as much to compensate for their negative experience and make them feel safe and loved again. Please do not be stingy regarding rewards and appreciating good behavior. Don't reserve praise just for significant achievements. Instead, praise even small day-to-day moments like putting the toys away or sharing them with their siblings.

Offer warnings when appropriate.

It would be unrealistic to skip all methods that require a little strict attitude. For example, sometimes children need a reminder about who is in the metaphorical driver's seat. However, instead of yelling, give warnings that you will follow through with if they do not comply. Saying, "If you don't complete your homework, you won't watch any TV today." is better than yelling because you make them realize that their actions have consequences.

Make it easier for them to comply.

Exhibiting good behavior can be a complex process. Hence, as a parent, you are supposed to make that process as easy as possible for your child. For example, imagine your children are having their dose of screen time, and you ask them to stop and get ready to go to bed. Chances are high that they will start nagging and get frustrated.

What if you give them a heads up that they could watch for ten minutes more after and then start the bedtime ritual? The same applies to almost anything; going out, visiting friends, getting ready to go to school, etc. By conditioning their minds for the upcoming task, you make it easier for them to comply.

Compromise whenever possible.

Parenting is exhausting enough that you do not want to make it any harder on yourself by hassling over minor details with your child. For instance, if they're going to wear their new shades to school on a rainy day with no sun in sight, don't fuss over it and come to a compromise so that both parties can win. Tell them they can wear them but will have to take them off in class. In this way, you are allowing them to have autonomy over small matters so that you can take up control over other important situations. Of course, you could argue with your child that the shades are a wrong choice since it is raining, but that will only drain you mentally and unnecessarily strain the relationship with your child. So, choose your parenting battles wisely and compromise as needed.

Keep your power.

Remember that you are in charge of the relationship with your child. When you argue with a defiant child, you are just indulging in the kid's fantasy that they have control over you and can challenge you. Unfortunately, with more arguments comes more frequent defiant behaviors. Instead of letting your child challenge you to a power struggle, refuse to participate in their relentless requests. You can even leave the room to make them realize that you will not engage in a conversation with them that takes your control away. Instead, use positive and negative reinforcement and explain the consequences of their behaviors to stay in charge. At the same time, please do not blame your child for their anger or defiance. They lack the essential cognitive skills to understand and express their emotions appropriately.

Encourage physical activity.

If your adorable little child is not looking so cute anymore since they're screaming at the top of their lungs, attempt to introduce more physical activities into their lives. Maybe they behave defiantly because they are cooped up at home and asked to do homework or household chores. Instead, take an interest in their favorite sports, provide the resources, and play with them. By doing so, you not only build a more healthy parent-child relationship, but you also provide the means to release their pent-up stress in a non-harmful way.

Do not negotiate.

Seeing your child scream and yell their head off can be jarring. You might freeze up when your mind is racing with all the strategies to approach to handle the situation but are unable to pick the best one. This indecisiveness could be overwhelming and make you give in. As a result, your child will associate their tantrums with your compliance and act defiantly to get what they want again since they know you will eventually give in. Sometimes, there won't even be a solid reason to act out, but they will do so because they want something out of you. If the parent does not give in to the child's demands, they will at least try to negotiate. Do not engage in this negotiation game! If you do that, you teach them that acting out will work. Instead, try to establish some ground rules at home and consequences if those rules are broken. We will discuss how to do this in more detail later on in this chapter.

Define the consequences clearly.

When disciplining your defiant child, leave no room for ambiguity and set clear, understandable consequences. For instance, "No ice cream you tonight until you clean up your room" presents a clear consequence with a defined duration. If you do not specify how long a consequence will last, your child will feel like you are being too strict and lose hope of improving themselves. Furthermore, the consequences you set should serve a learning purpose, not punishment. For example, if your child is refusing to get up from playing video games and do their homework, choosing not to let them play their favorite game ever again is harsh and more of a punishment for not complying than it is to teach them to comply. Instead, suppose you choose to present a more logical consequence, like not letting them play until they have done their homework. In that case, you will yield more results because you are encouraging good behavior by negative reinforcement (i.e., by removing an undesirable consequence in case of compliance). If you are not clear enough about what you expect from them, the consequence of incompliance, and how long it lasts, they will not feel compelled to follow along with the consequences. Finally, there is no point in setting up clear and concise consequences if you are not going to be consistent in implementing them. If you want your rules to be effective and result in positive behaviors on your child's part, you should be adamant in following the rules you have established. Behavioral reinforcement will not yield results if there are no consequences sometimes and many consequences the next.

Explain your expectations clearly.

When you are telling your child what not to do, for example, "Please don't run away from me in the grocery store, I get really worried", pair it with explaining what behavior you want to see instead, like "How about you hold my hand instead when we're in the grocery store?" By doing so, they can concentrate on practicing the positive alternative. This also teaches clear communication to your child, i.e., explaining their needs and feelings, just like you did.

Recognize and remind the good behaviors

When caught in a severe temper tantrum, it can be hard to see the good and positive behaviors your little one has exhibited. Hence, to parents angry with their children over their misbehavior, I always recommend sitting down and making a list of all the times your child did the right thing. You can even share this list with your kid when they have calmed down from their tantrum and discuss it with them. They will feel appreciated and praised and want to repeat the good actions to receive similar encouragement. This effective form of positive reinforcement works very well for most children and various age groups.

Speaking gently and respectfully takes you far.

If someone asks me harshly to do something difficult, I would not feel compelled to do that task. But, on the other hand, when asked nicely, I would feel encouraged to do even the most difficult tasks. Similarly, kids feel motivated to do better when they're talked to gently and with care. Hence, while they may not be reasonable and willing to listen during their tantrums, sit down with them after they have calmed down and discuss their behavior. Again, the key is to talk to them in the manner you would want them to speak to you; keep a calm and gentle tone, and discuss what behavior you expect from them. Under no circumstances curse or insult your child. You are their champion and role model. Just as your words of encouragement place them on top of the world, your insults will break them and ruin their self-esteem. So, never resort to expressing your anger through insults, and be mindful of what comes out of your mouth because while you may forget after some time, they never will.

Handle sibling squabbles with caution.

Taking care of one defiant Child is a task, but taking care of two or more children who have made it their moral obligation to push each other's buttons can prove highly grueling. While sibling squabbles can make up for some humorous moments, at times, it can only be a headache that needs to be dealt with immediately, but with caution. Suppose you are driving with your kids, and both of them fight over the last packet of chips. You can hear screams, struggles, and constant kicks at the back of your seat. You cannot ignore the situation in this case because it distracts you from driving and is very hazardous. So what are you going to do? Pick sides? No! With siblings, you should never pick sides and choose who is right or wrong. Instead, adopt a more responsive strategy. For example, stop the car whenever possible and authoritatively tell them to sort matters out between them because you will not budge unless they do. Doing so sets a precedent that you will not rush to save the day when they fight. Instead, they'll have to work together to devise a solution. Make them see the trouble they are causing you and how it can sometimes be perilous, and let them know their actions have consequences.

Be present in your child's life.

Lastly, none of the techniques mentioned above will work if you are not there for your child to talk about their feelings and listen to them. They depend on you to help them comprehend their emotions. So, you must acknowledge their feelings and be there for them in all your capacity. This way, you will create an environment that makes them feel seen and confident about your love for them. We all have moments when we are not as active or engaged in our child's lives. But those moments should be exceptions. As a parent, if those moments last longer and become the norm, you will start to fail. Your children will never return to their current age; maybe, when they are grown up, they do not like to be with you that much. So, if you want to be in your child's memories later, be in their lives today!

How can you be warm and involved with their lives and firm and consistent in setting expectations and enforcing limits? We will find out the answer in the next chapter on balanced parenting!

Chapter Six

Becoming a Better Parent

You can learn many things from children. How much patience you have, for instance.

Franklin P. Adams

Parenting starts with you! You need to be regulated (mentally, emotionally, and physically) before you can model regulation for your child. If you, as the parent, are stressed out, your mind is disturbed, or your emotions are out of control, you cannot connect with your child and be present for them. My experience with many foster kids and my son shows that balanced and positive parenting is difficult or even impossible without a balanced parent (mentally, emotionally, and physically). This chapter presents various strategies to become a better parent by creating balance in you (the parent). In my pursuit of balanced parenting, I have found the following two strategies especially helpful:

1. Reducing and managing stresses

2. Practicing mindfulness for parenting

These two strategies go hand in hand and complement each other. Following the general tenet of this book, we start with you (the parent), and in the next chapter, we focus on your Child's mental and emotional balance.

Before we move any further, let me clarify a critical point. It would be very naive to assume that parenting stress originates only in the parent or that all parents face the same challenges. External factors play a considerable role in the creation of parenting stresses. For example, the presence or absence of economic prosperity, family-friendly work policies, and social support can make or break parents in modern societies. Also, having a child with mental or physical health issues or a difficult temperament could be a constant source of stress. So, external factors matter tremendously. Some parents might be more fortunate than others. For example, they live in a country with family-friendly work policies, have support from close relatives, or simply have easy-going kids. Whatever situation you have, remember that parenting stress is not a measure of your worthiness and does not make you an inferior parent. Instead, it is a sign that you have too much to handle, and you better take some steps to eliminate or manage the stressors.

You experience parenting stress when you feel you cannot cope anymore. In other words, your mental, emotional, or physical resources are insufficient to meet your child or environment's demands. In such situations, the parents are less sensitive to their children and less capable of relating to their needs, thoughts, and feelings. When stressed out, there is a higher chance that parents turn to harmful response mechanisms to cope with the stress. They will either blow a fuse and overreact to their children or become unresponsive and withdrawn. The outcome is harsh, bossy, or emotionally disengaged parents. We know that stress is contagious; it gets into people around us, especially children. Stressed-out parents make their kids act as a coping mechanism, and the vicious cycle continues!

Parents usually have to multitask during some parts of the day, for example, when doing the evening chores, preparing dinner, to getting ready in the morning. When multitasking, we tend to lose our temper with our kids more easily. It makes us less attentive, increases our anxiety and stress, and makes us miss information. Moving back and forth between tasks while caring for a child could be stressful and exhausting for many parents. That is why I believe multitasking is a significant source of stress for modern parents, and we need to step away from it whenever possible to curb parenting stresses. In my experience, mindfulness, both on its own and in the parenting context, can help tremendously to become a more attentive and connected parent.

Parenting stress disrupts parent-child bonding, taking away emotional warmth and nurturing. In addition, it leads to a cascade of issues for both parents and children; parents feel guilty and worried, and children become less social and prone to anxiety and stress-related diseases. So, what can you do to tackle parenting stress? In the rest of this chapter, we will review various strategies to eliminate or reduce stress and explain how to use mindfulness to become a better parent.

Tackling the parenting stress

Like many parenting topics, there is no one-size-fits-all solution. Children are different; what works for one child might not work for another. However, we can draw some general principles that work for everyone by focusing on what is within our circle of control. First, we discuss seven tips to tackle parenting stress. Afterward, we will separately discuss mindfulness in the context of parenting. I have used all of these tips myself, have seen great results, and highly recommend trying them!

Address external stressors as much as possible.

Let's start with stressors not originating from you, for example, your working condition, your child's temperament, family situations, etc. As mentioned before, we cannot simply ignore such factors and pretend that stress is only about your mindset! It might be that you can do little to change the world around you. But, at least you will become more aware of your reality! So, start with identifying the stress sources; is your child keeping you up at night, too much workload, living costs, your relationship with your partner, etc.? Are you bringing stress from work to home? Once you have pinpointed the issue, check if you can change something, get help from family, friends, or co-workers, and make the change wherever possible. "What you're supposed to do when you don't like a thing is change it. If you can't change it, change the way you think about it. Don't complain." That is what Maya Aneglou said in her best-selling spiritual classic book Wouldn't Take Nothing for Journey Now. This might sound a bit disappointing, but it's true! Sometimes, we cannot change the world to our liking. That is when the next tip might help!

Use cognitive reframing.

Cognitive reframing shifts your mindset and encourages you to view a situation, person, or relationship from a different perspective. For example, imagine your child comes home from school exhausted and drained and rushes to their room without talking to you. Instead of thinking, "I am a terrible parent. My kid doesn't want to talk to me", adopt a much more positive mindset, "They must be exhausted to just go to their room like that." Reframing how you perceive a hurtful situation changes your emotional reaction by considering another reality to the case.

We get upset and stressed when our expectations do not match the realities of the world around us. For example, you expect your child to cooperate fully in a hurry. But you forget that your young child does not experience the world as you do and does not realize that you are in a hurry. When you fail to adjust your expectations or cannot reframe how you perceive situations, your mind will become your biggest stressor. Cognitive reframing helps parents bounce back from stressful experiences and makes it less likely for them to overreact and take counterproductive disciplinary measures.

Plan better and budget for more time.

Many people, especially high-performers, perfectionists, highly educated people, and those who demand a lot from themselves, would like to squeeze as many tasks as possible into their schedules, hoping to get more done. We usually underestimate the time needed for a task and put ourselves under time pressure and stress. The same could happen at home, for example, when preparing to drop the kids at daycare or school before going to work or leaving for an appointment. If running late drives you crazy, you should plan better and start earlier. Also, manage your expectation of how quickly children can act. They are usually slower than adults and need more time to think, learn, and react.

When you set a good to-do list, plan and start earlier, you have a higher chance of being on time and suffering less from time pressure and the subsequent stress. If you have young children, you cannot expect yourself to get as much done as you do without the heavy responsibility of raising one or more children. So, do yourself a favor; do not bite more than you can chew, plan better and start earlier to prevent time pressure and stress.

Do not forget to have fun.

Whenever things get tough with my foster kids, we plan a fun activity to diffuse the tension and bring everyone to a better mood. For example, we go to the movie theater, play board games, go to the zoo or museum, etc. When everyone feels better, it is easier to connect and correct behaviors. It also reminds us that we love each other and could treat each other with more love and understanding. So, do not wait for some "special moments" to enjoy some time with your children. Instead, do it whenever you can, especially when you cannot cope anymore.

Make a self-care plan.

Parents, especially those with young children, are usually so busy that they forget to care for themselves. The truth is the best way to take care of your family is to ensure you are healthy and happy. Otherwise, you will become angry, resentful, stressed, and unable to give good care to others. The critical point is that taking care of yourself is not selfishness. For example, if you spend time on a good message and pedicure instead of being with your child all the time, you are not being selfish. On the contrary, you do yourself and your family a huge favor. Time is a scarce and valuable resource for parents. Hence, they should carefully plan how and when to spend time on self-care. You can start by writing down what matters to you and what brings you joy. Of course, you might not engage in every item on your list. But you can at least take the top one (or ones), and think of when and how to do them.

Your self-care plan does not need to be fancy or include anything special. Even taking small chunks of time daily to reset and relieve stress will significantly help. Think of what works for you; yoga, meditation, watching movies, reading a book, listening to music, etc. Do not forget physical activities. Even simple activities such as walking or cycling can enormously help. Regardless of what you do, try to spend some time every day, so you can handle parenting challenges gracefully instead of feeling trapped and worn out.

Avoid overscheduling yourself and your child

You do not want your kids to miss out on opportunities to participate in extracurricular activities. That is understandable. However, signing your child up for too many activities could become counterproductive and stressful. The same applies to you, the parent. Feeling obliged to use your time every day and on the weekends as much as possible probably will not make you happier. Finding the right balance is not easy. The rule of thumb is whether you enjoy a particular activity. Do you have a good time with your child? Is it making your child happier? If not, maybe you should stop that activity or at least take a critical look at your schedule and how you spend your family time.

Build up your tribe.

It takes a village to raise a child, right? Unfortunately, many parents do not have a village to support their parenting. Social support is like a relief valve for parenting pressures. One of the best ways to get such support is by connecting with fellow parents. After all, nobody understands what you are going through as much as other parents! As your child grows and goes to daycare and school, you will come in contact with many potential friends (i.e., other parents!). As a general rule, try to talk to people as much as possible. This will increase the chances of finding like-minded parents. Start conversations without high expectations. Who knows, maybe a random chat is the beginning of a great friendship. Finding parent friends will help you (and your child) to be happier and get away from parenting stresses. So, reach out to other parents around you and build your tribe!

Practicing mindfulness for parenting

Does this scenario sound familiar to you? You are preparing dinner while checking your phone. Your daughter comes with a question about her homework, and your son shouts from upstairs, inviting you to go and see his latest lego creation. You are in constant motion, trying to manage everything. But then something goes wrong in the kitchen, on the phone, or in the corridor and sends you over the edge. You explode, and the whole evening is spoiled. Different versions of this imaginary scenario happen to many parents. In fact, such dramas are so common that we might think of them as an unavoidable part of parenting. But, if you think carefully, multitasking (in other words, dealing with more than one task at a time) and not your children make you lose your temper.

Multitasking is touted as a "skill," and many of us are proud to be multitaskers at work and home. However, according to research published by American Psychological Association, multitasking cuts productivity and efficiency. Task switching costs us time and mental energy, makes us miss information, increases the chances of making mistakes, and puts us under pressure and stress to reach multiple goals (i.e., finishing many tasks) simultaneously. The truth is multitasking is a necessary evil for most parents and cannot be avoided altogether. So, what can we do to manage the parenting responsibilities without getting worn out?

I have tried mindful parenting with excellent results. Mindful parenting is practicing mindfulness in the parenting context. It is stepping away from being a constant multitasker parent and trying to do things more attentively, preferably one at a time. Oxford Learner's Dictionary defines mindfulness as "a mental state achieved by concentrating on the present moment, while calmly accepting the feelings and thoughts that come to you, used as a technique to help you relax." For me, mindful parenting is being mentally present, at least during some parts of the day, especially while interacting with my children. I try to spend some time with them daily when I engage in nothing other than talking and playing with my children.

Furthermore, I try to have some quiet time for myself, doing yoga stretches in the morning and reading a book in the evening. My kids are happier and much more collaborative when I give them my full attention. Similarly, my quiet minutes in the beginning and the end of each day make me more relaxed and content. Being a mindful parent is not stopping multitasking altogether, doing yoga, and sipping late all day long. Instead, it is giving yourself a break, stopping feeling guilty for not making the most out of every moment, and being aware of the hidden costs of constant multitasking.

I started this chapter by saying that you need to be regulated (mentally, emotionally, and physically) before you can model regulation for your child. If you limit and manage your parenting stresses and be mindful of how you spend your day and interact with your child, you are on the right path to becoming a positive role model. In the next chapter, we will talk about how to go to the next level and teach emotional management to your child!

Chapter Seven

Raising an Emotionally-Intelligent Child

It is easier to build strong children than to repair broken men.
Frederick Douglass

Have you encountered parents who handle difficult parenting situations with calm and grace? They behave as if they can read their children's minds, readily communicate with them, and make them see the logic. Those parents possess a crucial skill set; the ability to recognize and manage their emotions while appropriately responding to their child's feelings. This is called *Emotional Intelligence (EI)*, also known as *Emotional Quotient (EQ)*. Dr. Daniel Goleman, the American psychologist, author, and science journalist popularized the term "Emotional Intelligence" in his 1996 book *Emotional Intelligence: Why It Can Matter More Than IQ*. He explains that EI is a learnable skill set we can cultivate at any age and outlines the following five components for it:

1. Self-awareness: knowing your emotions, motives, triggers, strengths, weaknesses, and how you impact those around you.

2. Self-regulation: the ability to control your impulses and reactions, thinking about the consequences before responding, and reacting proportionately to the given circumstances.

3. Empathy: the ability to understand how other people feel and relate to their experiences without judging them quickly.

4. Motivation: the innate drive for personal development and success without relying on external rewards like wealth or fame.

5. Social skills: the ability to readily interact with the people around you, for example, in a team, using eye contact, verbal communication, active

listening, and open body language.

All five components of EI (according to Dr. Goleman) are important for successful parenting, and some are essential. Unfortunately, weak EI (in children and parents alike) is the root cause of many parenting dramas. When children cannot recognize and communicate their emotions, they express them physically by throwing tantrums, frowning, screaming, stomping, fist-clenching, throwing objects, hurting themselves and the people around them, etc. Likewise, when parents are not emotionally intelligent, they are prone to parenting stress and unhealthy coping mechanisms.

As parents, we strive to instill good values in our children and build them up to become their best versions. But none of that is possible if they do not understand what to do with their feelings. An emotionally-intelligent child does not try to convey their message physically, has better relationships (with parents, teachers, and other children), is happier, and has a higher chance of success later in life. Therefore, EI is essential for parents and children and is a focus area in positive parenting. Emotionally intelligent parents consider their child's negative emotions and misbehaviors as teachable moments for themselves and their children. They also know that emotional understanding is like a moving and ever-changing target and requires flexibility and adaptability, for example, with different ages and temperaments. EI results from interactions between personal characteristics and environmental factors for both parents and children. So, EI depends on temperament, physical and mental health, parent-child interaction, educational system, and child-rearing practices. This chapter discusses the skills needed to support the development of your child's EI and how you can become an emotional coach for them.

Teach your child about feelings

As mentioned before, children lack the cognitive abilities to readily identify and understand the causes of their feelings. Even adults do not always know why they feel upset or angry, let alone young children! Your child will lash out if they do not understand why they feel a certain way. The situation worsens when the parent and child cannot communicate properly; the child lashes out to get the message across and express anger and frustration. So, when you tantrums, instead of getting frustrated in return and taking the misbehavior personally, understand that your child is only trying to get your attention. They need your emotional support and understanding and not blame and anger. You can help them, for example, by verbalizing their feelings: "I can see you're upset that your sister took your toy." Clarifying your child's emotions and frustrations helps the child to identify them and become capable of recognizing them in the future. With time you can amp up the vocabulary and go from sad, upset, angry to lonely, anxious, and frustrated. Also, remind your child (and yourself!) that feelings are temporary, like visitors that come and soon leave! This takes the severity of negative emotions away.

Take anger as an example. It is a normal emotion, and throwing tantrums is expected of growing children. So, don't feel alarmed if your child throws a tantrum from time to time. This is a stage of their development, but you must approach it correctly. However, a few general guidelines work with almost all children. The language parents use when dealing with angry and explosive children has a massive impact on them. "You keep lashing out even after I have told you a thousand times not to! You are such an angry child." Adopting a tone similar to this only makes the child feel as though they are at fault for how they choose to express themselves and that the problem is with them. By doing so, your child fails to realize that the problem is not that they are inherently a "bad" or "angry" child. Rather their anger – a perfectly normal emotion – is being channeled incorrectly. If you continue to call the problem and child as one, they will become overwhelmed by their anger and fail to manage it effectively.

Instead, what parents should do is externalize the anger that the kid is facing and identify it as the challenge that needs to be overcome. This benefits your child tremendously as they begin to separate themselves from the problem. In addition, treating these challenges as an external matter by giving them a name and even a face allows your child to manage their anger issues safely. Even simple statements like this can do wonders: "Recently, you are getting angry quite often. How about we sit down and spend some time naming and drawing that anger that you feel?'"

Children lean towards engaging and interactive activities, and if such activities help them cope and manage their emotions, then that's just killing two birds with one stone. One such creative method to tackle emotional instability is the anger iceberg. Since anger can be at the forefront of many other feelings, such as guilt or embarrassment, this metaphorical iceberg allows your child to understand how anger operates and what underlying emotions it is signaling. In addition, it will aid your kid become more aware of their feelings and how to address them.

This activity calls for the parent and child to spend time together and discuss how the child feels about something. For instance, how your little one felt when they were excluded from group play at the playground. While they must have reacted angrily initially, that is just the tip of the iceberg, and deep down, they may be feeling hurt, disappointed, and left out. By practicing this activity, you and your little one bond, allowing them to clear their head and understand that although they react angrily, the root causes of their anger are other feelings. Hence, the next time they face an unpleasant scenario, they will form a clearer image of how they feel and how to manage accordingly.

Validate your child's emotions.

Recognizing and validating your child's feelings sets up the safe and loving environment every child needs. Not only that, but by affirming their feelings, you are also painting yourself as a capable and trustworthy figure in their eyes; your child will begin to see you as someone they can turn to when the disappointment with life becomes too heavy to bear. Your child needs the proper guidance to understand their thoughts and emotions. Validating their experiences and emotions helps them achieve the emotional maturity to deal with their feelings effectively and independently. When you validate your child's experiences, you allow them to accept negative feelings just as much as positive ones. Furthermore, you teach them how to approach situations where they do not get what they want.

When your child comes home from school and starts spilling all the details of their day, focus on what they are saying and try to make them feel like you're genuinely paying attention. Keep your body language to show you are listening, whether sitting with them at eye level or nodding to their stories. For example, responding like, "Really? And then what happened?", can make your child feel like they're genuinely being heard and can say anything to you because they trust you'll listen. If your children get into a quarrel, listen to both parties impartially and validate how they feel, "I understand how upset you must feel because your brother broke your favorite toy." Such responses allow the child to see that you can relate to and understand their problems and treat them with the same urgency. While it may seem like a trivial matter, in their eyes, it is a big deal. Hence, their problems need to be dealt with with the same importance and not any different as it can make them feel alienated.

While children often cannot sufficiently understand their emotions, they can read your responses very well. Hence, it will not affect them if you blankly tell your child to "calm down" or "take it easy" and not with genuine compassion. Since, at times, you will feel like you are not able to relate to your child's problems, like a broken toy or lost shirt, in those times, focus on how you would have felt if you had misplaced something important. Then, take those feelings and approach your child with the same genuineness you want to be approached with. During meltdowns, parents should not resort to just telling them to "calm down". Simply telling them to stop feeling a certain way will not make them stop. Instead, it will make them think their emotions are unacceptable and that it is wrong to feel frustrated or upset. Instead of putting a premature end to your child's feelings, allow them to feel their emotions freely.

A common pitfall with many parents is that they minimize their children's feelings and even blame them for feeling that way. This happens, for example, when the parent says, "Don't get so mad over something so small!" or "Stop being so dramatic!" In vulnerable and sensitive moments when your child feels overwhelmed, they need someone to affirm them. Instead of saying, "Stop worrying about your shirt, you'll find it,"; say, "You must be so upset you lost your favorite shirt. Don't worry, let's look for it together". Doing so teaches your little ones to identify and deal with their feelings. You make them feel validated, that they are not wrong for feeling this way, and can feel safe with you.

Differentiate between emotions and behaviors.

Understanding the difference between emotions and behaviors is key to enhancing your child's emotional intelligence. Emotion is what we feel, and behavior is when we act on the feeling. So, for example, anger is a feeling. But hitting because of that anger is a behavior. Similarly, sadness is a feeling, and screaming out of sadness is a behavior. Your goal is not to suppress certain feelings in your child. Instead, you should teach them how to deal with uncomfortable emotions. For example, it is OK if your child feels angry. But throwing a tantrum out of anger is unacceptable. Since the human brain works with rewards and punishments, you can teach emotional management to your child by awarding or punishing their behaviors (i.e., using positive and negative reinforcements, as explained in Chapter Three), not their feelings. The main message would be that the child will not face the consequences of their emotions. But if they decide to express their feelings by misbehaving, it will be a different situation.

Set clear rules and expectations.

When teaching your child how to manage their feelings, it's essential to establish a balance of expectations from your child, not too high or too low. In this case, aiming for the stars is applicable here with a caveat. As parents, we want the best for our children and usually set very high expectations. However, if the bar is excessively high, it might appear that our children will only be appreciated and loved if they meet those very high expectations. This is a common parenting pitfall; to reward achievements, not effort or progress. If your little one took extra time to finish cleaning their room, recognize that effort and appreciate it, even if the job is not perfectly done. By doing so, you are teaching your child that even if they do not "reach the stars", you will still love and care for them just as much. This unconditional love creates a sense of emotional safety for them. By the way, do not turn your failures into life goals for your children. For example, if you failed to have a black belt in Karate, do not force your child to practice Karate. Maybe they do not like it at all!

Boundaries are your non-negotiable expectations. For example, it should be clear to the child that while it is OK to feel angry, they cannot physically hurt people or damage the objects around them. Crossing boundaries should have consequences; negative reinforcement or punishment. Remember to remind your child that the penalty is for their behavior, not their feelings. If your child cannot manage anger and cannot help but throw a tantrum at every inconvenience, you need to set up rules that encapsulate what you expect from them. For instance, zero tolerance for physical violence, name-calling, and lashing out by breaking whatever they can lift. By establishing such rules, you teach your child that regardless of their feelings, they can not react to their frustrations by causing destruction or wreaking havoc physically or verbally. Your goal in setting boundaries, rules, and expectation is to teach discipline and not to punish.

Be consistent.

Along with setting reasonable and balanced expectations, a parent must strive for consistency if they want to bear the fruits of balanced parenting. Unfortunately, parents are mostly unaware of the power of consistency in teaching emotional management skills. The more often you do something, the better results you will yield, and a similar is the case with teaching kids to manage emotions effectively. If you choose to react by disciplining your child when they act out on one occasion but then let it slide on another, you only confuse them by setting an uncertain precedent. Your child will not correct behavior unless they know how you will react. Teaching kids to do anything is no easy job, let alone teaching them to manage their emotions. It is a long and tiring process to rehearse expectations and model good behavior consistently. Consistently practicing emotional management and effective communication helps your child to feel more secure and less in need of acting out.

In addition, it models good behaviors without doubt and instills clear and effective decision-making later in life.]

Connect before correct.

Your go-to response to your child's aggressive behavior may be immediately saying "No" or "Stop that!". The tantrum will not magically disappear just by ordering your child to stop. Think about why children throw tantrums; they cannot handle their emotions, try to have your attention, push the boundaries, and see where you will give in. Unless you address these root causes, the tantrum will continue. Remember to connect before correct! Talk to your explosive child calmly and let them see why you are not getting them that toy. If you have set specific rules, review them again and remind your child about the boundaries. Give them your attention and help them calm down. You can use tantrums as productive, teachable moments.

You are effectively your child's emotional coach when practicing the abovementioned points. You help your child recognize and name their feelings, model emotional regulation for them, validate their behaviors, teach them all emotions are OK but some behaviors are not, and constantly enrich the parent-child connection. Over time, you will enable your child's intrinsic motivations for personal development, instill good values and habits, and help them become emotionally intelligent and well-rounded individuals.

In an environment where your little one feels heard and seen, they can look up to you and show trust and co-operation. Hence, establishing a solid parent-child connection should be your top priority. Start by being fully present for your child for short periods. Then create daily, weekly, or monthly rituals to do fun activities and create memorable moments together. Remember that neither you nor your child won't come back to this age and moment again! In the last chapter of this book, we will elaborate on enriching the parent-child connection, some parenting myths, and how to benefit from positive parenting to become more connected to your child.

Chapter Eight

Forming a Well-Knit Parent-Child Relationship

Tell me and I forget, teach me and I may remember, involve me and I learn.
Benjamin Franklin

In 1938, Harvard University started the Harvard Study of Adult Development to track the health and well-being of 268 Harvard sophomores, including President John F. Kennedy. The goal was to find clues to leading healthy, happy lives. After following the surviving men for more than 80 years, the world's longest study of adult life, researchers have found a treasure trove of data on the influence of heredity, environment, and individual actions and habits. Scientists eventually expanded the study to include the men's offsprings, now in their 50s and 60s, to understand how early-life experiences influence health and well-being. One of the conclusions from the second-generation study is the following: "Relationship is the secret to a happy and successful life. Having a childhood in which one feels accepted and nurtured is one of the best predictors of adult success, well-being, and life satisfaction." A similar decades-long study has been conducted in the UK. The "1970 British Cohort Study" follows the health and development of 17000 people born in England, Scotland, and Wales in a single week in 1970. The researchers in this study have found that the most potent childhood factor for adult life satisfaction is the child's emotional health.

Decades of scientific research show that having responsive, balanced, and engaged parents is vital to the emotional health of children. A nurturing parent-child relationship enhances the child's mental, emotional, and social health, creates a secure attachment, teaches emotional regulation, and lays the foundation for the child's personality, well-being, and future success. Staying connected with your child as you spend days in the parenting trenches does not happen unintentionally. It requires your continuous effort and consciousness. It is not easy, but it is definitely doable and certainly very rewarding. This final chapter builds on the previous learnings and provides new tips to help you create and maintain a solid and healthy bond with your child to become a better parent by the day. We will discuss five qualities of a healthy parent-child relationship, i.e., what to aim for, five misconceptions about the parent-child relationship, i.e., what not to believe, and five strategies to create and maintain a tremendous parent-child relationship, i.e. , what to do daily.

Five qualities of a healthy parent-child relationship

So, how can we define a good parent-child relationship if this relationship plays such a massive role in children's future success and well-being? In other words, strengthening which qualities should become your priority? Just like "perfect parenting" is not easy to define, we might have different options about what constitutes a good parent-child relationship. However, it is possible to think of some foundational elements desired in any good parental relationship. In my experience, the following five items are absolutely needed:

Honesty

Any good relationship should start with honesty from everyone involved. In a parent-child relationship, the easier part is that parents should not lie to their children. Maybe sometimes they don't tell the whole truth, but lying is never a good idea. The more challenging part is how to raise honest kids. Children lie to avoid trouble, get out of trouble, get what they want, etc. Being a truthful parent is a good starting point, but it is not enough. Kids need to know that they'll be better off or in less trouble if they tell the truth. Then, depending on how often and how badly they lie, you can take various actions, from ignoring if the lying is not severe or does not often happen to giving them a second chance to tell the truth or clarifying the consequences. Being a positive role model, i.e., being an honest parent, and incentivizing them to tell the truth (through positive and negative reinforcement) are your main tools to incorporate honesty into your relationship. Honesty is the foundation for the other qualities of a good parent-child relationship, such as trust. Let's talk about that in more detail.

Trust

Parents and children with healthy and positive relationships trust each other. They tell the truth and confide in each other to share thoughts and feelings. Trust is critical for kids to share their difficult experiences and negative emotions. It is also crucial to count on their parents' support and guidance. Trust makes children feel safe and willing to bond with their parents and communicate honestly. This will create a positive feedback loop that continuously nurtures the parent-child relationship.

Mutual respect

All parents hope their children will be respectful to them. However, since children usually mirror what they see and experience around them, you need to model being respectful to your children, for example, by respecting their opinions when they're different from yours, respecting their privacy, and of course, not lying to them. Parents often expect respect from their kids. However, respect should be reciprocal, starting with the parents. You are the role model, not them. You teach good behavior with your words and actions. When you care about their feelings and opinions, your children mimic that and return the same behavior. So, instead of expecting respect and blaming your kids if they fail to meet your expectations, please first pay attention to how you treat them. Parents who communicate well with their children, explain the boundaries, make agreements with them, accept their individuality, keep their promises, and remain consistent reinforce mutual respect with their children. I hope we all manage to have such a relationship!

Unconditional love

In the context of parenting, love is the warmth, affection, attention, comfort, support, acceptance, and nurture that children receive from their parents. Of course, we all love our children when they behave and make no mistakes. But what if they mess up or drive us mad? Will you still show the same affection, support, and acceptance? Unconditional love is not letting go of all rules and boundaries in the name of love. Instead, it is showing emotional support, especially when children make mistakes. Children need to know their mistakes do not determine whether they are worthy of their parents' love or not. Unconditional love is being consistently available to support your children and guide them in challenging moments of their lives. This gives them a sense of emotional safety, nurtures their trust in you, encourages them to explore the world, and strengthens their self-esteem.

Adaptability

Your child next year won't stay the same as today. Hence, your parenting should change too. This adaptability is essential to sustain a good parent-child relationship. In fact, without adaptability, you won't have a good relationship, even if you do everything else right. So solutions of today might not work in a few months. Similarly, what works for many others might not work for you and your child. So, wise parents are flexible and adapt their parenting practices to their child's evolution. They are also willing to revise their approaches if they don't work and are eager to test new ideas.

Five parent-child relationship myths

Understanding some of the parent-child relationship myths helps us to avoid them. This list is in no way exhaustive. However, these are the top five myths based on my experiences, and they probably apply to you too!

Parenting comes naturally!

If parenting comes naturally, what are all those shelves of parenting books for?! Are our instincts enough to raise happy and successful children in modern society? Can we teach our children self-esteem, emotional intelligence, problem-solving, communication, stress management, and many other skills without reading or following training on those topics? Parenting is hard. Good parenting (as defined throughout this book) is even harder and requires deliberate learning and practice. So if parenting comes naturally, why do we make wrong parenting calls so often? The idea that parenting comes automatically could be dangerous because it makes the parents who seek help doubt themselves. While very fundamental aspects of parenting could come naturally (e.g., how to keep a baby alive or safe!), there is so much we can learn about human psychology and child development that limiting ourselves to our gut feeling would be a big parenting mistake.

Good parents sacrifice their lives for their children!

Our modern culture encourages a very child-centric and child-obsessed lifestyle for parents. As a result, many parents ignore their own needs for their parenting duties. But how can you offer the best possible care and attention if you're not in good shape (physically, mentally, and emotionally)? Just like the airplane oxygen mask (put them on first before helping others!), you should first take care of your well-being before you can properly parent your child. Parenting could be so consuming that even your marriage or partnership can suffer. Parenting can reduce the marriage to a one-dimensional relationship, only about parenting and not a partnership or romantic relationship. Worn-out parents struggling daily in the parenting trenches could end up communicating only when there is conflict. Unfortunately, many marriages do not survive the neglect caused by the early years of parenthood. Good parents remain engaged with their children but also with themselves and their partners. They try to pursue a balanced life. This balance changes over time and is not the same for parents with newborns and teenagers. Once the first few intensive months after having a child are over, it is vital to return to a normal life where you can spend time with yourself and your partner and not get consumed by parenting.

Spend more time together, and you'll be fine!

In my pursuit of better relationships with my children, I've found and used many pieces of parenting advice. But to my surprise, sometimes seemingly great pieces of advice did not work or even worsened the situation! For example, spending more time or eating family dinners together is fantastic parenting advice, right? But after a few attempts, I gave up because it did not help at all. When I started reflecting on this experience, I realized that spending more time together helps only when the parent-child relationship is already good. If spending time together could always improve the connections, we should all have perfect relationships with our children during the pandemic lockdowns!

When a relationship is damaged, trying to improve it by being together more often is like trying to fill a bucket of water with a big hole! Spending more time together is useless without addressing the root cause of the poor parent-child relationship. So, before you wear yourself and your child down with forced togetherness, think of what you've learned so far and see if you are the essential parenting good practices (your stress management, being a positive role model, responsiveness to your child, etc.) in place.

You can spoil your child with too much love!

We defined parental love earlier in this chapter. Parents show their love when they kiss, hug, praise, or compliment their kids or when they are responsive, attentive, or supportive of their children. To assess the role and value of parental love, we should consider what happens without it. Unloving parents are indifferent, unaffectionate, or neglecting at best, hostile, aggressive, and abusive at worst. Without parental love, children will feel neglected or rejected. The myth is that "too much" parental love is harmful, i.e., parenting should be a bit "tough." However, apart from how one would define "too much" parental love, scientific studies show that strict parenting produces kids with lower self-esteem and more frequent non-compliant behaviors. Without parental love, parents tend to become either neglectful or strict. In either situation, children do not learn to internalize self-discipline. In addition, kids raised by authoritarian parents have higher tendencies toward bullying, aggression, and depression. Children, like all humans, are hardwired to be loved. With a healthy relationship with your child, you can relate to them positively, not punitively. Love is the language of connected parenting. When you practice parental love to connect to your child, be attentive to them, teach them skills, and build their self-esteem, there is no limit to how much they can benefit from your love.

Disciplining equals punishment!

Punishment and blame are the most accessible tools to damage the relationship with your child. As mentioned in the previous chapter, most parents think of discipline as punishing their children when they misbehave, not teaching them or modeling good behavior. Imagine you decide to spank your child because of their behavior. Wouldn't they wonder why it's OK for you to hit them but not for them to hit their siblings or friends? Wouldn't that team them that aggression is OK to reach their goals? Chapter 3 reviewed various reward systems to positively or negatively reinforce behaviors. Unfortunately, many parents mix up negative reinforcement with punishment. While they intend to reinforce a behavior negatively, they end up punishing their child and miss the reinforcement aspect altogether. Disciplining is much more than punishment, and corporal punishment is definitely unacceptable. So next time you need to discipline your child, please consider what you've learned throughout this book (especially in Chapter 3) and use discipline to model good behaviors and reactions.

Five strategies to connect to your child

So, how can parents establish a healthy and strong connection with their children? I think the ingredients are surprisingly simple and common sense. That doesn't mean implementing them is easy! Nevertheless, if you can get these fundamental building blocks in order, you have a great chance of success:

Build trust and respect.

Establishing a great parent-child relationship starts with building trust and respect. I have experienced this firsthand, especially with some of my foster kids who had a complicated past and struggled with trusting people. But this is important for all parent-child relationships. Trust and respect go hand in hand, especially when children grow older. You can nurture trust and respect in your relationship in many different ways. Here are some examples:

- Keep your promises: This is a no-brainer; if you promise to buy them something or be present for their school event, try your best to keep the promise.

- Be available when they need you: Imagine how it feels when a child needs care, help, or support. But the parent is not there to provide for them. The child will naturally lose trust and believe they cannot count on the parent.

- Respect your differences: As children grow, they start to have preferences and opinions, sometimes entirely different than yours. You can build trust by listening to them without judging and helping them if they ask for it. Don't force your preference on them. For example, maybe you like martial arts. But they like football. Of course, this aspect of your relationship evolves with your child's age and is not the same when they are 7 or 15 years old. You can allow your child to make some harmless decisions at younger ages. However, they will become more demanding as they grow older, and the differences could become more evident.

- Set clear rules and expectations: This is like signing a contract with your child, in which

both parties know their roles and responsibilities. When you set rules and define the consequences of breaking them, clarify your expectations, explain what your child can expect in
return, and keep practicing them consistently,
your child can count on your word and learn
from your behaviors. This is real trust-building.

- Let the relationship evolve and adapt: Parent-child relationship is a living, dynamic phe-
  nomenon. Over time, you and your child
  change, and so should the terms of your relationship. For example, they love you to be
  around them when they are 7. But that will
  probably change when they are 15. So, be flexible enough to adapt to their changing needs.

I always think of parent-child trust this way: Imagine
your child has messed up and needs help. Do you prefer
them to think, "Let's go to daddy or mommy for help!"
or "Don't go to mom or dad, they will get mad at you!"?
I prefer the former answer! How about you?

Be present for them.
Being 'present in the moment is more than being physically around your kids. It is paying attention to what goes
on with your child, their thoughts, behaviors, feelings,
worries, and needs without judging or giving directions.
If your child likes to pretend that the Lego pieces are
people, play along with them. If they want to tell you

everything that happened at school today, listen patiently and in an engaging way. They usually like to lead the play. So, let them take the lead, and you follow and respond. In Chapter 6, we talked about mindfulness and how stepping away from being a constant multitasker parent can help you experience less stress. The same concept can help you connect better to your child. For example, setting aside just 10 minutes a day to talk to your child without distractions can make a difference. So turn off the TV, put away your electronic devices, and spend quality time together. The quality of your presence and communication is crucial to establish a positive relationship. Being distraction-free is essential, but not enough. Young children tend to talk a lot, sometimes about random topics! Think of yourself as a therapist when listening to your child. Try to listen patiently, engagingly, and without judging.

Shower your child with love and attention.

As discussed earlier in this chapter, spoiling your child with too much love is a parenting myth. Humans are hardwired for love. When children feel they aren't getting enough attention, they will throw a hissy fit to get your undivided time. On that note, if you're showering your child with love, care, and attention, they won't go through the trouble of lashing out when they can simply come up to you for all their parental love needs. If you shower your children with affection, they become less likely to defy and misbehave and more sure of themselves.

They won't need to look elsewhere to meet their needs for love and attention. As a result, you can form a much deeper and richer connection with your child. Your child must receive gentle, caring touch (i.e., hugs) from you several times throughout the day. Treat every interaction as an opportunity to connect with your child. Greet them with warm expressions, give eye contact and a smile, and tell them daily that you love them. Love them unconditionally, even if you're mad at them because they failed an exam, dislike their behaviors, or are annoyed by them. An emotionally intelligent parent knows that these feelings are temporary, could create teachable moments, need appropriate and proportionate reactions, and is nowhere as important as the bond with their child.

Share activities together

Sharing activities is a fantastic way to bond with your child, whether it is reading books, playing, cooking, gardening, sports, visiting museums, painting, or doing science experiments. Depending on their age, there are so many bonding activities. Kids love feeling included, even as simple as bringing the dishes to the dinner table or adding the cake topping. Reading to your child not only instills a good habit but also makes reading books with you their favorite activity of the day. They will look forward to bedtime because they get to listen to you narrate their favorite book. In addition, reading to your child will allow you two to bond over fictional characters and plot lines.

Parents should make the parenting process as interactive and engaging as possible. For example, I encourage my children to put on a play about something that happened to them in real life or something entirely fictional. Then, I help them prepare for the show if needed and get engaged as much as they like. During this process, I am mentally and physically present. We practice communication and problem-solving and learn how to handle differences of opinion. Some say playing is the science of childhood. When children play together, they learn to plan, solve problems, communicate, and manage emotions. We can practice the same skills by playing alongside our kids. Nothing can help you build deep and positive relations with your child better than making memories and having fun while playing together. Let them have their way if your child prefers free and unstructured play. What matters is to have a joyful and energizing time together. Playing together allows you to know your child and their preferences better. This will, in turn, help you to better engage with them in the future and further enrich your bond.

Reflect and let go!

You might be one of those parents who spend a lot of time analyzing their kids' misbehavior and comparing them with their peers and friends. Then, they search for the root causes in their child as if the child is the sole source of their parenting issues. We are almost at the end of this book, and by now, a few points should be clear:

- Children are not mature enough to process all their emotions.

- They mimic the behavior of the people around them, especially their parents and caregivers.

- Parents are their children's role models.

- Parenting starts with you and continues with the relationship with your child.

So, it's likely that what children express is simply a reflection of what they see and experience from the world around them, most notably from you!

As soon as you realize this critical point, you will shift your attention inward and start reflecting on your words and actions. Parenting is not a solo game. It is more like a tango between the parents and the child, with the parent in the leader role! When you stop blaming your child, unconditional love for them will be more accessible, and your bond will strengthen.

Summary

We started with an introduction to positive parenting and why it can work for all families, especially for raising explosive and easily-frustrated children. In the first two chapters, we discussed why children show oppositional and defiant behaviors, how parental mistakes magnify the defiance, and how to avoid such mistakes. Chapter 3 reviewed various reward systems to reinforce behaviors and how to correctly implement positive and negative reinforcement in the context of positive parenting. We also compared and contrasted reinforcement with punishment.

Many parents experience frustration when repeatedly telling their children what to do and how to behave with no positive outcome! On the other hand, children rarely forget to mimic what their parents do. After all, we are their role model! Chapter 4 was about playing this imitation game. Children observe actions and reactions and reflect on them like a mirror. For example, if you're expressing frustration by lashing out or choosing to yell and become distant when faced with difficulties, so will your kid. But this mirror effect also creates learning moments for your children; they can copy good behaviors from you and forget their misbehaviors because of how you act and talk. The reward system will come in handy here, so recognize and reward good behaviors and remind them about the undesirable ones.

Chapter 5 was about yell-free parenting and how to implement it to reduce or eliminate the harmful effects of psychological aggression. The guardian-child dynamic places the guardian in a position of control and power. A yelling parent is not in control. It's OK to be upset, but parents in control communicate their anger or frustration in more controlled ways, such as explaining the consequences or giving options to diffuse the situation. They always speak gently and respectfully, are present and involved, and compromise or let go if needed.

As mentioned on several occasions in this book, parenting starts with you! You need to be regulated (mentally, emotionally, and physically) before you can model regulation for your child. If you, as the parent, are stressed out, your mind is disturbed, or your emotions are out of control, you cannot connect with your child and be present for them. Chapter 6 reviewed various strategies to eliminate or reduce parenting stress and how to use mindfulness to become a better parent. If you limit and manage your parenting stresses and be mindful of how you spend your day and interact with your child, you are on the right path to becoming a positive role model.

As parents, we strive to instill good values in our children and build them up to become their best versions. But none of that is possible if they do not understand what to do with their feelings. Chapter 7 focused on developing Emotional Intelligence (EI) and discussed the skills needed to support the development of your child's EI and how you can become an emotional coach for them. Emotionally-intelligent children do not try to convey their message physically, have better relationships (with parents, teachers, and other children), are happier, and have a higher chance of success later in life. Therefore, EI is essential for parents and children and is a focus area in positive parenting. In the book's last chapter, we elaborated on enriching the parent-child connection. Furthermore, we reviewed some parenting myths, and how to benefit from positive parenting to become more connected to your child.

To wrap up, let's review the most important takeaways of this book in a nutshell:

- Positive parenting focuses on the child's strengths rather than their weaknesses. The central thought is to have positive and instructive interactions with your child and to offer warmth, empathy, and support.

- Positive parenting works for everyone because it focuses on fulfilling children's basic emotional needs of attention and power.

- Positive parenting is proactive; you take action

to ward off future misbehaviors. When you address your children's need for attention and power regularly and positively, you minimize the instances in which they try to fulfill their emotional needs by misbehaving.

- Parenting starts with you. Your child adores and mimics you, you are their role model.

- You should be emotionally regulated before you can teach emotional regulation (the airplane oxygen mask concept). So, don't forget to take care of yourself.

- A healthy relationship with your child should include caring, teaching, leading, communicating, and striking a balance between being firm and compassionate.

- Be flexible and adaptable as your child grows and their needs change.

- Parents are defined by their mistakes. Positive parenting helps you survive inevitable parenting blunders, bounce back, and keep going!

I hope Positive Parenting for the Explosive Child becomes your guide to adopt a yell-free parenting lifestyle to establish a safe and loving environment for your child or children. If you enjoyed this book, please submit a review to help future reader like yourself and me as a writer. Thank you and good luck!

Selected References

Chapter 1

- Fanning, J. R., Meyerhoff, J. J., Lee, R., & Coccaro, E. F. (2014). History of childhood maltreatment in Intermittent Explosive Disorder and suicidal behavior. Journal of Psychiatric Research, 56, 10–17. https://psycnet.apa.org/record/2014-28591-002

- Weishaupt, J. (2021, December 13) What Is Intermittent Explosive Disorder? WebMD. Retrieved July 29, 2022, from https://www.webmd.com/mental-health/what-is-intermittent-explosive-disorder

- Nickerson, A., Aderka, I. M., Bryant, R. A., & Hofmann, S. G. (2012). The relationship between childhood exposure to trauma and intermittent explosive disorder. Psychiatry Research, 197(1–2), 128–134. https://doi.org/10.1016

/j.psychres.2012.01.012

- Janoff-Bulman, R. (1992). Shattered assumptions: Towards a new psychology of trauma. APA PsycNet. Retrieved August 20, 2022, from https://psycnet.apa.org/record/1992-97 250-000

- Greene, R. W. (2014). The explosive child a new approach for understanding and parenting easily frustrated, chronically inflexible children. Harper.

- Clarke-Fields, H. (2020). Raising good humans: A mindful guide to breaking the cycle of reactive parenting and raising kind, confident kids. New Harbinger Publications.

- Miller, M. (2021). The uncontrollable child: Using Dbt skills to parent a child with disruptive moods and emotional dysregulation. New Harbinger Publications, Inc.

- Dobson, J. C. (2017). The new strong-willed child: A completely revised and rewritten guide taking you from birth through adolescence. Tyndale Momentum, the nonfiction imprint of Tyndale House Publishers, Inc.

Chapter 2

- Hostile, Disobedient and Defiant Behavior in Children. (2019, December 3). Yale Medicine. Retrieved August 19, 2022, from https://www.yalemedicine.org/conditions/defiant-children

- Miller, C. (2022, February 8). How to Handle Tantrums and Meltdowns. Child Mind Institute. Retrieved August 19, 2022, from https://childmind.org/article/how-to-handle-tantrums-and-meltdowns/

- Canady, V. A. (2019). APA policy calls spanking harmful discipline for children. Mental Health Weekly, 29(8), 7. https://doi.org/10.1002/mhw.31790

- Greene, R. W. (2014). The explosive child a new approach for understanding and parenting easily frustrated, chronically inflexible children. Harper.

- Clarke-Fields, H. (2020). Raising good humans: A mindful guide to breaking the cycle of reactive parenting and raising kind, confident kids. New Harbinger Publications.

- Miller, M. (2021). The uncontrollable child: Using Dbt skills to parent a child with disruptive moods and emotional dysregulation. New Harbinger Publications, Inc.

- Dobson, J. C. (2017). The new strong-willed child: A completely revised and rewritten guide taking you from birth through adolescence. Tyndale Momentum, the nonfiction imprint of Tyndale House Publishers, Inc.

- Siegel, D. J., & Bryson, T. P. (2012). The whole-brain child: 12 revolutionary strategies to nurture your child's developing Mind. Bantam Books.

Chapter 3

- Daniels, A. C. (2016). Bringing out the best in people: How to apply the astonishing power of positive reinforcement. McGraw-Hill Education.

- Ackerman, C. E. (2022, June 20). Positive Reinforcement in Psychology (Definition + 5 Examples). PositivePsychology.Com. Retrieved August 27, 2022, from https://positivepsychology.com/positive-reinforcement-psychology/

- Gibeault, S. M. (2018, October 23). 4 Tips for Training Your Dog With Rewards. American Kennel Club. Retrieved August 27, 2022, from https://www.akc.org/expert-advice/training/training-rewards/

- Jarocha, T. (2022, July 14). Angry Kids: Dealing With Explosive Behavior. Child Mind Institute. Retrieved August 27, 2022, from https://childmind.org/article/angry-kids -dealing-with-explosive-behavior/

- Maggin, D. M., Chafouleas, S. M., Goddard, K. M., & Johnson, A. H. (2011). A systematic evaluation of token economies as a classroom management tool for students with challenging behavior. Journal of School Psychology, 49(5), 529–554. https://doi.org/10.1016/j.jsp.2011. 05.001

- Shrestha, P. (2019, June 16). Operant Conditioning. Psychestudy. Retrieved August 27, 2022, from https://www.psychestudy.com/behavior al/learning-memory/operant-conditioning

- Trach, E. Examples of Positive Reinforcement. YourDictionary. Retrieved August 27, 2022, from https://examples.yourdictionary.com/ex amples-of-positive-reinforcement.html

- Why Parents Shouldn't Use Food as Reward or Punishment - Health Encyclopedia - University of Rochester Medical Center. (n.d.). University of Rochester Medical Center. Retrieved August 27, 2022, from

https://www.urmc.rochester.edu/encyclopedia
/content.aspx?ContentTypeID=160&Content
ID=32

- Clarke-Fields, H. (2020). Raising good humans:
  A mindful guide to breaking the cycle of reactive
  parenting and raising kind, confident kids. New
  Harbinger Publications.

- Payne, K. J., & Ross, L. M. (2020). Simplicity
  parenting. Ballantine Books.

- Siegel, D. J., & Bryson, T. P. (2012). The
  whole-brain child: 12 revolutionary strategies to
  nurture your child's developing Mind. Bantam
  Books.

Chapter 4

Northwestern Medicine Staff. (2015, May 6). Being
the Best Role Model. Northwestern Medicine. Retrieved
September 1, 2022, from https://www.nm.org/healthb
eat/healthy-tips/being-the-best-role-model

- Gibson, L. C. (2015). Adult children of emotionally immature parents: How to heal from
  distant, rejecting, or self-involved parents. New
  Harbinger Publications, Inc.

- Purvis, K., & Qualls, L. (2020). The connected
  parent. Harvest House Publishers.

- LaVigne, M., & Freitas, I. (2020). Play therapy activities: 101 play-based exercises to improve behavior and strengthen the parent-child connection. Rockridge Press.

- Siegel, D. J., & Bryson, T. P. (2016). No-drama discipline: The whole-brain way to calm the chaos and nurture your child's developing Mind. Bantam Books.

Chapter 5

- Wang, M.-T., & Kenny, S. (2013). Longitudinal links between fathers' and mothers' harsh verbal discipline and adolescents' conduct problems and depressive symptoms. Child Development, 85(3), 908–923. https://doi.org/10.1111/cdev .12143.

- Straus, M. A., & Field, C. J. (2003). Psychological aggression by American parents: National data on prevalence, chronicity, and severity. Journal of Marriage and Family, 65(4), 795–808. https://doi.org/10.1111/j.1741-373 7.2003.00795.x

- Martin, B. P. (2016, May 17). The 5 C's of Effective Discipline: Setting Rules for Children.

Psych Central. Retrieved September 3, 2022, from https://psychcentral.com/lib/the-5-cs-of-effective-discipline-setting-rules-for-children#2

- Siegel, D. J., & Bryson, T. P. (2016). No-drama discipline: The whole-brain way to calm the chaos and nurture your child's developing Mind. Bantam Books.

- Siegel, D. J., & Bryson, T. P. (2012). The whole-brain child: 12 revolutionary strategies to nurture your child's developing Mind. Bantam Books.

- Faber, J., & King, J. (2017). How to talk so little kids will listen: A survival guide to life with children ages 2-7. Scribner.

- Naumburg, C. (2019). How to stop losing your sh*t with your kids: A practical guide to becoming a Calmer, happier parent. Workman Publishing.

- Markham, L. (2015). Peaceful parent, happy kids: How to stop yelling and start connecting. Perigee Book.

Chapter 6

- Anger management: 10 tips to tame your temper. (2022, April 14). Mayo Clinic. Retrieved September 4, 2022, from https://www.mayoclinic.org/healthy-lifestyle/adult-health/in-depth/anger-management/art-20045434

- Baumrind, D. (1967). Child care practices anteceding three patterns of preschool behavior. Genetic Psychology Monographs, 75(1), 43–88.

- Brockman, R., Ciarrochi, J., Parker, P., & Kashdan, T. (2016). Emotion regulation strategies in daily life: mindfulness, cognitive reappraisal and emotion suppression. Cognitive Behaviour Therapy, 46(2), 91–113. https://doi.org/10.1080/16506073.2016.1218926

- Control anger before it controls you. (2022, March 3). American Psychological Association. Retrieved September 4, 2022, from https://www.apa.org/topics/anger/control

- Naumburg, C. (2019). How to stop losing your sh*t with your kids: A practical guide to becoming a Calmer, happier parent. Workman Publishing.

- Leyland, A., Rowse, G., & Emerson, L. M.

(2019). Experimental effects of mindfulness inductions on self-regulation: Systematic review and meta-analysis. Emotion, 19(1), 108–122. https://doi.org/10.1037/emo0000425

- Clarke-Fields, H. (2020). Raising good humans: A mindful guide to breaking the cycle of reactive parenting and raising kind, confident kids. New Harbinger Publications.

Chapter 7

- Goleman, D. (1996). Emotional intelligence: Why It Can Matter More Than Iq. Bantam B ooks.Brackett, M. (2020).

- Permission to feel: The power of emotional intelligence to achieve well-being and success. Celadon Books.

- Gottman, J. M., Declaire, J., & Goleman, D. (2015). Raising an emotionally intelligent child. Simon & Schuster Paperbacks.

- Siegel, D. J., Hartzell, M. (2018). Parenting from the inside out: How a deeper self-understanding can help you raise children who thrive. Scribe Publications.

- Lantieri, L. (2014). Building Emotional Intelligence: Practices to cultivate inner resilience in children. Sounds True.

- Kanoy, K. (2013). The everything parent's guide to emotional intelligence in children: How to raise children who are caring, resilient, and emotionally strong. Adams Media.

Chapter 8

- Siegel, D. J., Hartzell, M. (2018). Parenting from the inside out: How a deeper self-understanding can help you raise children who thrive. Scribe Publications.

- Clarke-Fields, H. (2020). Raising good humans: A mindful guide to breaking the cycle of reactive parenting and raising kind, confident kids. New Harbinger Publications.

- Siegel, D. J., & Bryson, T. P. (2016). No-drama discipline: The whole-brain way to calm the chaos and nurture your child's developing Mind. Bantam Books.

- Purvis, K., & Qualls, L. (2020). The connected parent. Harvest House Publishers.

- Delahooke, M. (2022). Brain-body parenting: How to stop managing behavior and start raising joyful, Resilient Kids. Harper Wave, an imprint of HarperCollins Publishers.

- Stiffelman, S. (2012). Parenting without power struggles: Raising joyful, resilient kids while staying calm, cool and connected.